Also by John P. Cann:
*Counterinsurgency in Africa: The
    Portuguese Way of War, 1961–1974*
*Brown Waters of Africa: Portuguese
    Riverine Warfare, 1961–1974*

Co-published in 2013 by:

Helion & Company Limited
26 Willow Road
Solihull
West Midlands
B91 1UE
England
Tel. 0121 705 3393
Fax 0121 711 4075
email: info@helion.co.uk
website: www.helion.co.uk

and

30° South Publishers (Pty) Ltd.
16 Ivy Road
Pinetown 3610
South Africa
email: info@30degreessouth.co.za
website: www.30degreessouth.co.za

Copyright © John P. Cann, 2013

Designed & typeset by SA Publishing
    Services (kerrincocks@gmail.com)
Cover design by Kerrin Cocks

Printed for Helion & Co. by Henry Ling Ltd.,
    Dorchester, Dorset and for
    30° South Publishers by Pinetown
    Printers, Durban, South Africa

ISBN (UK) 978-1-909384-63-7
ISBN (SA) 978-1-920143-81-7

British Library Cataloguing-in-Publication
    Data
A catalogue record for this book is
    available from the British Library

Front cover: Flechas prepare to board a
helicopter after many days in the field.
Photo Fernando Farinha

CONTENTS

GLOSSARY

aldeamento	controlled settlement established by the Portuguese to protect the population	GRAE	*Governo da República de Angola no Exílio* or Government of the Republic of Angola in Exile
ANC	African National Congress		
assimilado	mostly a *mestiço* who was legally assimilated into Portuguese culture	*guia*	identity card
AU	African Union	MANU	Mozambican African National Union
		mestiço	mixed race person
cacimbo	a part of the rainy season characterized by heavy mist	*metrópole*	Continental Portugal
		miliciano	reserve officer
canhangulo	primitive firearm made with a water pipe for a barrel	MPLA	*Movimento Popular de Libertação de Angola* or Popular Movement for the Liberation of Angola
CCE	*Companhia de Caçadores Especiais* or Company of Special Hunters		
chana	a vast plain characterized by high grass	NATO	North Atlantic Treaty Organization
chefe de posto	head of post		
CIA	Central Intelligence Agency	OAU	Organization of African Unity, now the African Union
CIO	Central Intelligence Organization		
CIOE	*Centro de Instrução de Operações Especiais* or Centre of Instruction for Special Operations	PAIGC	*Partido Africano du Independência da Guiné e Cabo Verde* or African Party for the Independence of Guiné and Cape Verde
CMIG-Zero	*Centre Militaire d'Instruction Guerrilla-Zero* or Military Centre of Instruction in Guerrilla Warfare	PIDE	*Polícia Internacional de Defesa do Estado* or International Police for the Defence of the State
DGS	*Direcção Geral de Segurança* or General Directorate for Security		
		SCCI	*Serviço de Centralização e Coordenação de Informações* or Centre for the Centralization and Coordination of Intelligence
EEC	European Economic Community		
ELNA	*Exército de Libertação Nacional de Angola* or Army of National Liberation of Angola	SIGINT	signals intelligence
EPLA	*Exército Popular de Libertação de Angola* or Popular Army for the Liberation of Angola	SWAPO	South West Africa People's Organization
		ultramar	Portuguese overseas provinces or colonies
FARP	*Forças Armadas Revolucionárias de Povo* or Revolutionary Armed Forces of the People	UDENAMO	*União Democrática Nacional de Moçambique* or National Democratic Union of Mozambique
flagelação	a spray of machine-gun fire	UNAM	*União Nacional Africana Moçambique* or Mozambican African National Union
Flechas	indigenous troops, initially Bushmen in the east of Angola	UNAMI	*União Nacional do Moçambique Independente* or National Union of Independent Mozambique
FLING	*Frente de Luta pela Independência da Guiné* or Front for the Struggle for the Independence of Guiné	UNITA	*União Nacional para a Independência Total de Angola* or National Union for the Total Independence of Angola
FNLA	*Frente Nacional de Libertação de Angola* or National Front for the Liberation of Angola	UPA	*União das Populações de Angola* or Union of the Angolan People
FRELIMO	*Frente de Libertação de Moçambique* or Front for the Liberation of Mozambique		
fuzileiro	Portuguese marine	ZANU	Zimbabwe African National Union
		ZAPU	Zimbabwe African People's Union
GE	*Grupos Especiais* or Special Groups	ZIL	Eastern Intervention Zone
GEP	*Grupos Especiais Páraquedistas* or Special Groups Parachutists	ZIN	Northern Intervention Zone
		ZML	Eastern Military Zone
GEPC	*Grupos Especiais de Pisteiros de Combate* or Special Groups of Combat Trackers		

INTRODUCTION

The origin of my interest in the Portuguese campaigns in Africa began during the period between 1987 and 1992, during which time I was assigned as a naval officer to augment the staff of the NATO command, Commander-in-Chief Iberian Atlantic Area, in Oeiras, Portugal, for its various maritime exercises. All the Portuguese officers with whom I worked had fought in Africa during the Portuguese campaign to retain its empire between 1961 and 1974. The stories of their experiences during this lengthy 13-year war fascinated me, and even today it remains a conflict that is not well known or understood outside of Portugal and of which little has been written in English. My subsequent assignments generated an interest in insurgency and, as a consequence, I naturally returned to the Portuguese African campaigns when I had the opportunity to do so.

This volume is about the particular indigenous force known as the *flechas*, or 'arrows', that was established in 1966 in response to an intelligence-gathering need in the east of Angola. The Portuguese intelligence apparatus required specialized augmentation in Angola, and the national security police, known for the acronym PIDE, was designated to perform these counterinsurgency duties. PIDE faced initial problems in adjusting to the new environment and to gathering intelligence on the insurgents' movements. The population continued to be terrorized, the local situation remained confused, and there was a consequent pressing need for a long-term solution. PIDE continued to experiment with this uncertain situation in its search for the key. One obstacle to its efforts was the diversity of languages spoken, as there are perhaps 15 different dialects. By about 1967, in an attempt to make its reconnaissance missions more effective, it had begun to use local auxiliaries with their knowledge of the immediate terrain, familiarity with the population, and unique language skills. This initiative proved partially successful.

This use of auxiliaries began around the city of Luso in eastern Angola, and employed people who were born and raised there to go into the familiar bush and discover what was happening. These locals could travel easily through the country for extended periods, blending with the population and maintaining a low profile. Initially, these agents were simply supposed to observe and collect information on insurgents; however, PIDE found that they were being captured and tortured, so it began to arm them for their own defence and train them properly. It soon discovered that the Bushmen were best suited for this purpose. These people inhabited the vast remote area of the Cuando Cubango district in southeastern Angola, which was also aptly named '*Terras do Fim do Mundo*' (Lands of the End of the Earth). It is here that the Bushmen lived and were largely employed, and it is here that the Flechas began.

Flechas operated either independently or as part of a larger, formal force. They were devastating in spartan, low-profile, independent operations. These reconnaissance missions were wide-ranging, deep-penetration patrols in known or suspected enemy areas. Likewise, they developed great competence in joint operations with other, formal ground forces. In these situations they reported not to PIDE but to the local army commander and were used with their superior tracking skills to guide regular troops. The ground forces also relied on the Flechas to maintain the continuity of local operating knowledge in an area, as the overall experience level of a typical unit tended to degrade with the constant rotation of its troops.

Flechas were organized into combat groups along the same lines as the army and received extensively modified training, as Flechas always seemed to have a unique African way of solving problems. Their groups never exceeded thirty men, and they invariably operated in areas where they were familiar with the language and terrain. In the beginning in 1966 there were eight Flechas, and by 1974 there were upward of 1,000. This is the story of their rise to fame for their unequalled competence and effectiveness during wartime and their disappearance with the general cessation of conflict in southern Africa in the late 1980s. It is an inspiring tale of a gifted, dedicated, and loyal people betrayed by both Portugal and their new nationalist governments.

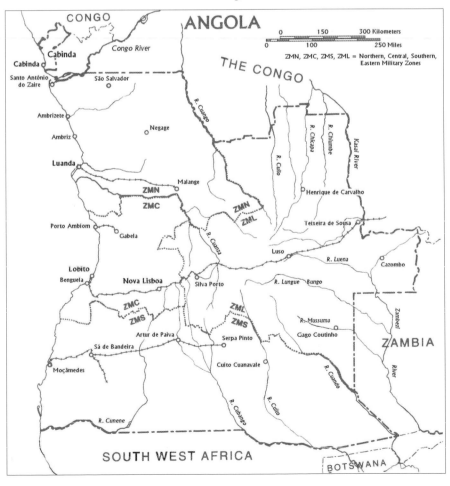

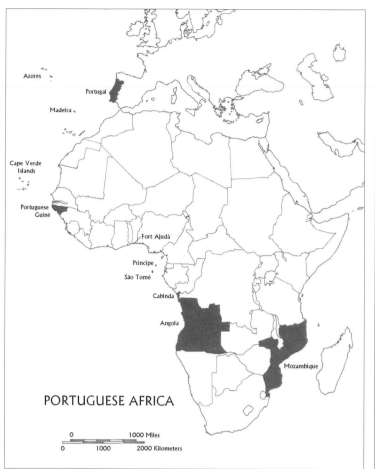

PORTUGUESE AFRICA

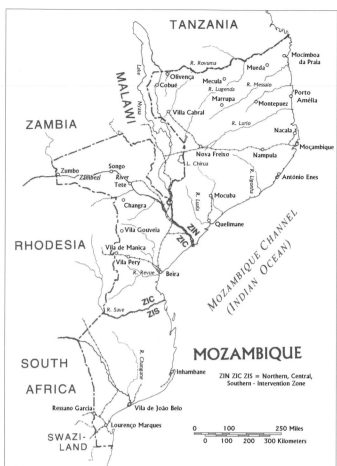

ZIN ZIC ZIS = Northern, Central, Southern - Intervention Zone

MOZAMBIQUE

PORTUGUESE GUINÉ

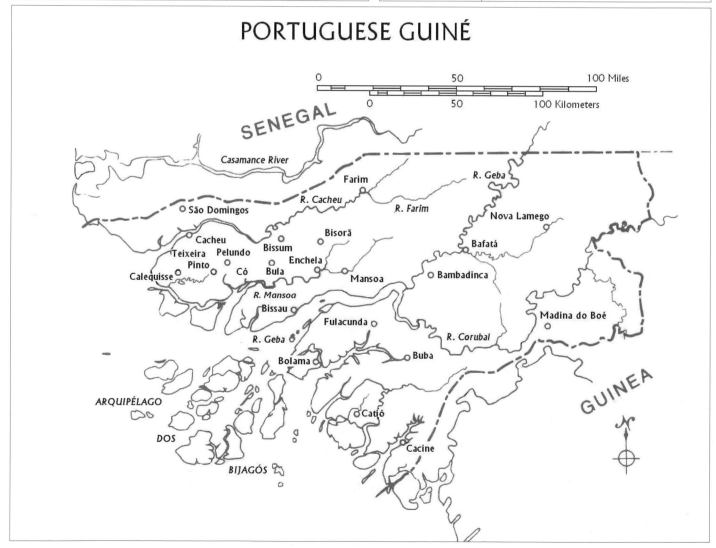

CHAPTER ONE:
PORTUGAL'S WAR IN AFRICA

In 1961, Portugal found itself fighting a war to retain its colonial possessions and preserve the remnants of its empire. It had been in Africa for over four and a half centuries, longer by far than any other colonial power, and its notion of the permanence of its empire drove it, with its modest resources, to defend its overseas provinces, or *ultramar*, at all costs. From its founding as a nation in the 12th century, it had had its back to a hostile Spain, a situation that foreclosed any land connection to greater Europe. Hence, it was forced to look seaward for its prosperity and initially found it in the Indian Ocean and later in Brazil – and on the eve of the wars in 1961, potentially in the African colonies, although the latter remained largely unfulfilled. Nevertheless, these African possessions were viewed as a vehicle for the renewed greatness of a former era and, as such, attracted a commitment beyond any previously demonstrated economic value.

This earlier era began in 1497, when Vasco da Gama rounded the Cape of Good Hope, discovered Mozambique, and established trading contacts in India. The trade was immensely profitable, and wealth poured into Portugal on an unprecedented scale. The Portuguese overcame the challenges of their new discoveries and proceeded to establish a systematic arc of enclaves strategically ringing the Indian Ocean that commanded both the sources of trade, as well as the sea routes themselves. As the Portuguese secured their dominance in this area, so localized trading profits, as well as those from the Cape route, increased accordingly, and propelled Portugal to the height of its power and influence. Its decline can be marked from June 1578 and its disastrous North African campaign designed to dominate the overland trading routes between the Gulf of Guiné and the Mediterranean. In a four-hour battle at Al-Ksar al-Kebir, King Sebastian and his army were destroyed by Moroccan forces.[1] The might of Portugal was wasted with this disaster. Portugal was never able to regain its 16th-century stature, and from that period until 1961 it experienced an irregular path of decline, with episodes of partial recovery. When Spain annexed it in its depleted state between 1580 and 1640, its overseas trade collapsed, and when Portugal recovered its independence, it was a wonder that it retrieved so much of its overseas holdings, particularly Brazil. As spices were the single-most lucrative commodity of the 16th century, so Brazilian sugar was in the seventeenth. When West Indian sugar became a competitive threat, gold was discovered in Brazil in 1694. In 1728 diamonds were discovered. The revenue from this colonial wealth maintained the continuity of Portuguese prosperity until Brazil became independent in 1822.

It was the recent memory of Brazil, and the wealth that it had provided, that generated a 20th-century hope for a similar colonial-led prosperity. On the eve of the wars, the two colonies of Angola and Mozambique were perceived as potentially modern-day Brazils and the prized keys to renewed prosperity and greatness. For this small European nation, the importance of the colonies was captured in an editorial by Marcello Caetano in *O Mundo Português* (Portuguese World) that appeared in 1935: "Africa is for us a moral justification and a *raison d'être* as a power. Without it we would be a small nation; with it, we are a great country."[2] This notion was reflected in a Portuguese map that overlaid Europe with the Portuguese possessions.

Colonial resistance

As colonial commitment was strengthening, so too was local resistance to it within the African population. Concurrently, Britain and France were freeing their colonial possessions in step with the post-Second World War trend. This development put increasing pressure on Prime Minister António de Oliveira Salazar to move in line with the Western European forms of government and allow the Portuguese colonies to do so as well. Political crises in the form of serial colonial revolts and the Second World War enabled Salazar to preserve the status quo and his personal regime. Consequently, nationalist resistance had the effect of reinforcing the Portuguese commitment rather than the opposite.

The nationalist movements that challenged colonial ownership had their origins in the 1930s and began with the practices of Salazar's New State (*Estado Novo*) repressing any form of dissent, particularly political. This attitude extended from continental Portugal, or the *metrópole*, to the colonies, or the *ultramar*. Resistance began slowly, as there were practical barriers to any such opposition in the ethnic and social fragmentation of the African community. Without strong leadership, it could not coalesce against the Salazar regime.

Local African grievances were long-standing and had come to the fore during the early 20th century with the influx of white settlers and abusive labour practices. This indigenous resentment was publicly evident in 1931 when an independent Mozambican newspaper, *O Brado Africano* (The African Roar) slipped through Salazar's censorship and published a scathing editorial titled 'Enough'.[3] Thereafter this feeling was never far below the surface, and the apparent calm was illusory.

Following the Second World War, nationalist sentiments grew among the *mestiços* (mixed-race peoples) and *assimilados* (mostly *mestiços* who were legally assimilated into Portuguese culture); however, these groups were largely urban and thus did not represent the greater population. As they were located in cities, they were in a hostile environment for two reasons: the majority of their opponents, the white population, lived in cities, and the national police, or PIDE (*Polícia Internacional de Defesa do*

The Portuguese empire overlaying Europe.
Photo Força Aérea Portuguesa

António de Oliveira Salazar, prime minister of Portugal.

Estado, or International Police for Defence of the State), operated most effectively there. Consequently, they were either short-lived or dormant.[4] By 1956, the young Marxists of the Angolan Communist Party contributed to the formation of the MPLA (*Movimento Popular de Libertação de Angola*, or Popular Movement for the Liberation of Angola). The MPLA developed roots among the urban and largely radical intellectuals of Luanda, among its slum dwellers and, to a lesser extent, eastward from the capital among the Mbundu and the Chokwe people. These urban roots were composed largely of *mestiços*, who controlled the party. The movement had little in common with the rural peasants of the north, east, and south of Angola and made little effort to gain their loyalty. This lack of proselytizing would give security forces an upper hand in later campaigns. In December 1956, the MPLA published its manifesto in a direct challenge to the government. Predictably the PIDE reacted adversely, and a number of MPLA leaders were forced to flee into exile. From 1957 onward PIDE action was so effective "that the nationalists were not able to maintain more than the most rudimentary organization inside the colonies and could not communicate with those cells that did exist".[5] The parties were forced to conduct their affairs from neighbouring states and were deeply influenced by their foreign connections. As PIDE systematically wrecked the MPLA organization within Angola, it became progressively weaker and isolated from its leadership that was now abroad.

The MPLA in exile established itself initially in Léopoldville in the Belgian Congo and aligned itself not only with other independent African nations and their socialist philosophy but also with the communist bloc. The leadership was consequently familiar with the communist theory on wars of national liberation, and organized itself accordingly. The MPLA found itself in competition with the other prominent Angolan nationalist group resident in Léopoldville at the time, the UPA (*União das Populações*

de Angola, or the Union of the Angolan People), for acceptance as the leading representative of the Angolan people. In 1962 the MPLA formed its military wing, EPLA (*Exército Popular de Libertação de Angola*, or Popular Army for the Liberation of Angola), to project its influence into Angola. This nascent force numbered between 250 and 300 young men who had undergone military training in Ghana and Morocco. The EPLA sought to expand the conflict with this force across the northern Angolan border and penetrate the entire country, publicizing the MPLA manifesto. Recruiting proved difficult because of ethnic rivalries, and military action was thwarted by the competing UPA. The UPA through its influence with the Congo leadership forced the MPLA to leave Léopoldville in 1963 and re-establish itself in Brazzaville in the French Congo, from which it was difficult to conduct a campaign across a hostile Congo and into Angola. As a result, northern Angola proved to be barren, and it was not until 1966, with the opening of the second front from Zambia, that some success would come.

The UPA was formed by Barros Nekaka in the mid-1950s from a number of small groups with conflicting goals. In 1958, Nekaka passed leadership to his nephew, Holden Roberto. UPA strength rested in the rural populations of the Bakongo ethnolinguistic region. These people straddled the northern Angolan border and occupied a contiguous area that included parts of the Belgian Congo, Angola, Cabia and the French Congo. It was the footprint of the ancient Kongo kingdom. Roberto unequivocally held the view that not just a 'Bakongo kingdom' or some other entity but that all of Angola must be freed of Portuguese rule. An ardent anticolonialist, Roberto was born in Angola but had lived his adult life in the Belgian Congo. He had been educated by the Baptist Church missionaries and employed in the Belgian colonial economy as an accountant, between 1941 and 1949. Northern Angola was an area that had become more politically aware in the 1950s through white settlement, Baptist missionary influence,

Northern border post between the Congo and Angola.
Photo Cesare Dante Vacchi

Holden Roberto

and easy access to the developing political activities of the Belgian Congo. Roberto thus professed to feel a close kinship with the Angolan peoples immediately across the border. The UPA was able to develop a following there because of the relatively open frontier and sparse Portuguese presence, and this loyal cadre became the basis for the uprising in March 1961. Portuguese authority in the area took the form of *chefes do posto* (heads of posts) and administrators, as opposed to the police presence of PIDE, and these officials were so sparse that it was physically impossible for them to maintain anything but the most casual control over their districts.[6]

While Roberto was relatively well-educated, he was a member of the Bakongo ethnolinguistic group, was not a *mestiço*, and consequently did not share the more European cultural perspective of the MPLA. He was also tribally oriented in contrast to the non-tribal declarations of the MPLA. As a result, the personality and leadership philosophy of the UPA contrasted clearly with the MPLA and its sophisticated *mestiço* leadership, which was left-wing, intellectual, and acculturalatively Portuguese. Funding and support also contrasted glaringly, as the MPLA was linked with the Eastern bloc. The UPA received financial support from the American Committee on Africa and from various African governments, preponderantly that of Léopoldville.[7] Accordingly,

they were never able to resolve their differences and indeed were unyielding competitors for the future spoils of Angola.

When the Belgian Congo became independent on 30 June 1960, its new government began giving Roberto practical assistance, including permission to establish a radio station and a training camp within its borders. This sanctuary was an important facet of early UPA operations. Roberto had witnessed the long series of Congolese crises that had begun with the violent political rioting on 4 January 1959 and that had led to the accelerated Belgian push toward Congo self-government and independence in 18 months. By December 1960, he believed that, just as the Belgians had quickly grown weary of armed conflict, so too would the Portuguese when it was initiated. He intended to use his Congo sanctuary and the porous common border to launch his revolution and remove Portugal from Angola.

The UPA formed its military wing, the ELNA (*Exército de Libertação Nacional de Angola*, or Army of National Liberation of Angola), in June 1961 after the March attacks had failed to achieve a Portuguese withdrawal. Roberto was its commander-in-chief and its other two leaders were Portuguese army deserters, Marcos Xavier Kassanga, its chief of staff in Léopoldville, and João Batista, its operational commander in Angola, with headquarters near Bembe. This leadership was ineffective. The "fiery-tongued"

ELNA troops drilling at Kinkuzu.

Roberto was so autocratic that he would accept little more than arms and money.[8] Indeed, he appeared hard, introverted and even sinister from behind his apparently ever-present sunglasses, which he seemed to wear even in dark rooms and on cloudy days.[9] The South African Defence Force vice-consul in Luanda, Brigadier Willem S. van der Waals, noted that without leadership and training, the ELNA "set a demoralizing example of politico-military incompetence and indiscipline ... [and] ... involved itself in military activities in the narrowest sense ... but avoided contact with the Portuguese security forces as far as possible."[10]

UPA behaviour in the March 1961 attacks certainly reinforced this appraisal, and René Pélissier estimates that the actions of both Portugal and the UPA in the nine months following the *jacquerie* drove over 150,000 refugees into the Congo.[11] Other estimates put the figure much higher at 250,000, and Alex Vines even estimates the figure to be as high as 400,000.[12] Van der Waals observes that the UPA lost an important opportunity, as it had neglected to indoctrinate, organize and win recruits among these refugees while they were in the Congo.[13] When they began returning to Angola in 1962, Portuguese propaganda and social work among them persuaded most to move into controlled settlements, or *aldeamentos*. This development deprived the insurgents of popular support, and their military action consequently occurred in a human desert. Portugal denied the UPA access to the population and foreclosed its ability to proselytize, as in a classic insurgency, and alternatively the UPA focused on preventing competitive infiltration by the MPLA. Accordingly, neither the UPA nor the MPLA were able to develop a robust internal political infrastructure in Angola. Portugal gained the upper hand and dominated the human terrain until 1974 in a classic example of successful informational warfare backed by civil support under a security umbrella.

The ELNA was a reflection of Roberto's ineffective leadership. Its training was so poor that despite its eventual expansion to about 6,200 troops, their deportment at such camps as Kinkuzu in the Congo was cause for alarm.[14] Andreas Shipango, South West Africa People's Organisation (SWAPO) representative in Léopoldville, made an appraisal during a 1963 visit: "With representatives from a number of other liberation movements, I visited Holden Roberto's training camps near the Angolan border with a view to sending our young men there. But the atmosphere in Roberto's training camps was very bad, and I could not recommend such a course."[15] Roberto had a weak military arm and an ineffective political message that Angola should be an independent country with him as its head of state. The approach proved totally ineffective.

This lack of direction caused great rifts in the UPA leadership. Despite the UPA reorganization in March 1962 at the behest of Joseph-Déseré Mobutu, who was head of the Congolese armed forces at the time, to include additional groups, to rename itself FNLA (*Frente Nacional de Libertção de Angola*, or National Front for the Liberation of Angola), and to establish a government in exile named GRAE (*Governo da República de Angola no Exílio*, or Government of the Republic of Angola in Exile), little of substance was accomplished. A frustrated Jonas Savimbi, Roberto's 'foreign minister' and an Ovimbundu, formally broke with the UPA/FNLA in July 1964, labelling Roberto a "corrupt racist", and eventually formed the third nationalist movement in Angola, UNITA (*União Nacional para a Independência Total de Angola*, or the National Union for the Total Independence of Angola). Savimbi publicly announced his break at the 1964 OAU (Organization of African Unity, now the African Union) meeting in Cairo, and alleged that Roberto had set up a "commercial empire in the Congo" and that FNLA administrators were "wage earners and profiteers who enriched themselves on the money of New York financial circles and other international organizations".[16] Within two years, Savimbi had built his meagre 12-man force into a sizeable army, gaining popularity and support as the only leader to work within the country alongside his men in battle against

Joseph-Désiré Mobutu and Mrs Mobutu, 1971   Jonas Savimbi, head of UNITA   Eduardo Mondlane, head of FRELIMO

the Portuguese. "Leaders must fight alongside the people and not stay abroad, sending second-class fighters to face the Portuguese," Savimbi proclaimed as he denounced Roberto.[17] While Roberto was renowned for his aloofness, the bearded Savimbi mixed often and easily with ordinary people, as well as his military.

The next year Alexandre Taty, UPA/FNLA 'minister of armaments', after challenging Roberto in an unsuccessful coup, defected to the Portuguese in Cabinda with a substantial number of his followers.

Roberto seemed more interested in personal power than in a war of national liberation and, according to US intelligence sources, was "subservient" to Mobutu, who protected him from internal challenges to his leadership.[18] As the Portuguese weekly *Expresso* observed in 1974, "The FNLA is Holden Roberto and Holden Roberto belongs to Mobutu, to whom he is connected by an umbilical cord."[19] Mobutu was playing both ends against the middle by loudly proclaiming his support for the UPA/FNLA, while discreetly cultivating good relations with Portugal, for, like Zambia, the Congo depended on the Benguela Railroad (CFB), which carried more than half its foreign trade. There were also dissident elements in Angola that, if unleashed in cross-border operations, could make considerable trouble for him. Consequently, he kept tight control over the UPA/FNLA activities both within the Congo and without. He provided just enough political and material support to give it international credibility and to provide the Congo with a stake in Angola should the Portuguese eventually leave.[20] As for Roberto, after 1966 he started a property business in Léopoldville and was often seen driving a shiny black Mercedes-Benz about the city, just as Savimbi had predicted. He clearly became less interested in running a nationalist movement and, according to US intelligence, had not set foot inside Angola since 1956.[21] As Henry Kissinger observed at the time, "The strength of the FNLA continues to suffer from Holden's refusal to move from Zaïre (the Congo) to Angola to take direct control of FNLA activities."[22] Indeed, Roberto

spoke French and English far better than Portuguese.[23] CIA Luanda station chief at the time, Robert Hultslander, later wrote that, "This organization was led by corrupt, unprincipled men who represented the very worst of radical black African racism … It was a squalid spectacle: a corrupt leader dancing to the tune of a foreign master."[24] As for his troops, they have been described as "underfed, ragged, and villainous" and were hardly a credible army.[25] The Portuguese, it seems, had little to fear from Roberto and his organization after the March 1961 attacks.

Aside from Angola, there were nationalist movements associated with Guiné and Mozambique that, prior to the events of 1961, were hoping to negotiate concessions with the Portuguese on self-determination. In Guiné efforts by local nationalists to organize began in the early 1950s. The PAIGC (*Partido Africano da Independência da Guiné e Cabo Verde*, or African Party for the Independence of Guiné and Cape Verde) was founded in September 1956 by local *assimilados* and educated Cape Verdeans led by Amílcar Cabral. Its initial political organization prompted an aggrieved dockworkers' strike on 3 August 1959, which ended in a violent disaster when it was broken with excessive military force. Fifty workers were killed, and the incident became known as the 'Pidjiguiti Dock Massacre'. PAIGC leadership quickly realized that peaceful protest would not achieve its objective of self-rule and independence. Accordingly, it shifted its strategy to one of clandestinely organizing the rural population for an insurgency.[26] PAIGC had learned hard lessons in 1959 well ahead of the MPLA and UPA/FNLA experiences of 1961, and had shifted its approach. It was not prepared to begin an insurgency in Guiné until January 1963, when all the elements for success were in place, including firm sanctuaries in adjacent countries.

The driving force behind the PAIGC was Amílcar Cabral, who was born in Guiné of Cape Verdean parents. Cabral was an agronomist by profession, was educated in Lisbon, had served the Portuguese administration in Guiné (1952–1955) and had worked for various agricultural institutions in the *metrópole* (1955–59) with research trips to Angola. His political awareness came at an early age and matured during his academic time in Lisbon. While influenced by Marxist-Leninist ideas of the time, Cabral was primarily a nationalist and developed his own variant of both the PAIGC political message and its associated military dimension.

He became quite attuned to the requirement for population indoctrination and keenly aware of the need to bridge the gap between the urban intellectual and the traditional Guinean. His two-year preparation of the political battlefield was classic in its effort to draw the population together in a common ideology that would transcend tribal and ethnic divisions. His investigation into local grievances was the most thorough of any of the nationalist movements.

Following the unsuccessful employment of autonomous guerrilla groups in the first year of the conflict, Cabral held the Cassacá Congress in February 1964, to reorganize the war effort and establish a national army, the FARP (*Forças Armadas Revolucionárias de Povo*, or Revolutionary Armed Forces of the People). Without Portuguese negotiations, Cabral's only option was to win in the field. He thoughtfully assembled and implemented the proper elements of an insurgency, particularly those related with political indoctrination, to achieve PAIGC ends.

In Mozambique there were several exiled, very small, nationalist organizations prior to 1961. The Portuguese government made every effort to dampen the spirit of nationalism in its formative stages; however, there were at any one time perhaps half a million Mozambicans, or about ten per cent of the population, working in several neighbouring countries. This group was exposed to new political ideas and, in the period 1958–60, they began to organize themselves into various associations with the goals of social contact, self-help and, ultimately, national politics. These were united in September 1962 in the wake of the 1961 Casablanca Conference, and at the urging of Julius Nyerere, the Tanganyikan leader, into FRELIMO (*Frente de Libertação de Moçambique*, or Front for the Liberation of Mozambique), making it the strongest and most important movement.

Eduardo Mondlane assumed its leadership, and it is thought that he was selected by Nyerere while he was teaching at Syracuse University in the United States. He, too, absorbed the lessons of 1961 and was not prepared to launch a guerrilla war until some three years later, in September 1964, after his small force was trained. Mondlane, in arriving late for the nationalist fight, was strongly influenced by the trends in Angola and Guiné. His organization initially developed along similar lines to the PAIGC and experienced the same sort of problems in subordinating military operations to political leadership. In fact, his doctrine paralleled that of the MPLA

Amílcar Cabral, head of the PAIGC

Pidjiguiti Dock, Bissau, 1966. *Photo Foto Serra, Bissau*

and particularly of the PAIGC, with its emphasis on political indoctrination, and it was along these lines that he sought to conduct his military campaign. Mozambicans had already tried peaceful demonstrations with the same consequences that had occurred in Angola and Guiné. At Mueda, on 16 June 1960, there was an attempt to petition the local Portuguese administrator, who responded by using troops against unarmed peasants. Reputedly 17 Africans were killed in this demonstration.[27] This apparent massacre politicized the Makonde people, who straddled the Mozambican-Tanzanian border, and affected the development of FRELIMO and its campaign, as FRELIMO now felt that armed struggle was the only answer. Portugal had clearly shown that it would not grant self-determination and would destroy those who demonstrated for political freedom.[28]

Peasant populations are not normally a revolutionary force, and such was the case in Portuguese Africa.[29] They are conservative by nature and find security and comfort in the routine of their lives and the socio-economic institutions that govern them. Change is resisted and outsiders are viewed with suspicion. The insurgents of the several nationalist movements in Angola represented change that the population was not prepared to accept readily. Thus, despite the justified grievances of the black African Portuguese citizens, by and large they appeared loyal to Portugal and suspicious of the activities of the nationalists. This apparent support reinforced the colonial commitment. As Portugal entered 1961, its internal confidence in its position was as strong as ever. A series of events occurred that had the cumulative effect not only of reinforcing this attitude but of hardening it into an irreversible course of war. These events began with the affront of the attacks in the north of Angola and continued with an attempted coup against Salazar in an effort to moderate the country's position toward the demands of the nationalist movements. This failure, alongside the message from the United Nations, served to silence moderate voices. The final blow was the débâcle of Gôa which made any further loss unthinkable.

March 1961 uprisings

The March assault served as a warning of things to come and prompted Portugal to think more clearly about defending its colonies. European troop strength in Angola numbered under 1,000 in early 1958, and was reinforced to about 3,000 by mid-1960.[30] Overall strength by the time of the assault was 8,000, of which at least 5,000 were African troops.[31] These forces, while scattered throughout Angola, were confined to garrisons in the larger towns and were accustomed merely to administering subjective rule.[32] This modest order of battle was neither properly organized, nor trained and led, nor adequately manned to face the uprisings of March 1961. Nor was it prepared to fight a counterinsurgency, the war Portugal would have to fight.

On 15 March 1961, the UPA launched a multipronged attack in northern Angola with a flood of 4,000 to 5,000 armed men across a 300-kilometre strip. This mob laid waste to whatever was in its path. Portugal was shocked at the horror, and Roberto's belief that

The UPA uprising: a destroyed farm and murdered workers.
Photo Arquivo Histórico Militar

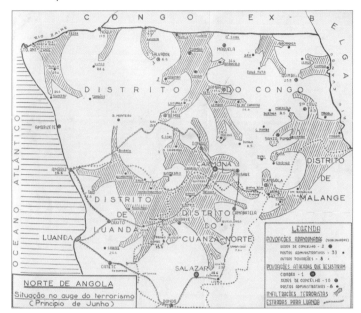

Attacks in the north of Angola at their height in June 1961. The arrows represent UPA infiltration routes. *Photo Hélio Felgas*

Portugal would capitulate at the first sign of violence, as Belgium had done, proved false.

This savage foray occurred in an area demarcated by the Congolese frontier, the Cuango River, the Malange-Luanda railroad, and the Atlantic Ocean. The attackers almost reached the capital, Luanda. Portuguese military leaders faced a situation in which over 100 administrative posts and towns in the three districts of northern Angola, from the Congo border to within 30 miles of Luanda, had been either wiped out, taken or paralyzed by the UPA. The economy of northern Angola was crippled. Communications were largely cut or damaged. Finally, thousands of Portuguese refugees were now camped in Luanda or were on their way back to Portugal where their arrival provided a chilling image of the dimensions of the disaster. The chaotic internal situation in Angola was rapidly and sensationally projected to a large international audience over the succeeding months.[33]

For a month Portugal and Angola seemed paralyzed and unable to act, aside from isolated naval and air actions. Equally, the insurgents were incapable of sustained military engagement, as their organization and logistic lines of communication were undeveloped. Civil militias were formed, and loyal Africans were armed to fend off the onslaught. It was this patchwork of civil-military defence and its frenetic activity that brought UPA momentum to a halt. Formal military reoccupation began in mid-May and was intensified as troops arrived from the *metrópole*.

The UPA assault was a senseless act of violence with only a naïve political aim, rather than a carefully considered military campaign with a political goal. Roberto's lack of understanding was reflected in his comment, "This time the slaves did not cower. They massacred everything."[34] This indiscriminate terror did enormous damage to Portuguese government credibility and deeply shocked the entire country. It also hardened the colonial commitment. To the Portuguese it was unthinkable that such lawlessness should be tolerated, and a strong, uncompromising reaction to the nationalist behaviour was widely supported. These events, with their resultant horror, also served to divert domestic attention from Salazar's increasing political vulnerability.

'Abrilada'

A fissure within the Salazar government was plainly evident when, on 17 February 1961, the US ambassador to Portugal, Charles Burke Elbrick, lunched with General Botelho Moniz, the Portuguese Minister of National Defence. The ambassador recorded that the general was very frank in his criticism of the Salazar regime and the impracticable and undesirable maintenance of the *status quo* in Portuguese Africa. He indicated that action must be taken to accelerate social reforms, both in the *ultramar* and the *metrópole*, and to "pry loose the iron grip of the few controlling families" over Portuguese affairs.[35] Moniz here claimed that he had discussed this position with the senior members of his staff, all of whom were in agreement, and that at least 90 per cent of the Portuguese armed forces supported this view. With "startling candor" he described Salazar's increasing inability to exercise true leadership and attributed this shortcoming to his advancing years.[36] Elbrick's final observation on the meeting was that Moniz was a man to watch.

The colonies were seen by many as a liability, in that their ownership under the current arrangement represented a major obstacle to Portuguese membership in the European Economic Community (EEC) and in trading with Third World nations, a direction that held great promise.[37] The strength of this view was manifested in the attempted coup of 13 April 1961, which was probably the closest that Salazar came to being removed. The 1960 débâcle in the Belgian Congo prompted heated debate in the Portuguese Supreme Council for National Defence (*Conselho Superior de Defesa Nacional*) about the security of its overseas territories, as there were clear limits to Portugal's ability to defend the *ultramar*. Colonel Kaúlza de Arriaga vigorously argued that the *ultramar* forces should be augmented, particularly in Angola.[38] He was opposed by Moniz and by fellow colonels Almeida Fernandes and Costa Gomes, who advocated a dose of the 'winds of change' for the colonial situation.[39] Moniz consequently undertook to write a long, formal and well-meaning letter to Salazar, describing the concerns that he and many of his politico-military colleagues on the Council shared about a military solution to the colonial

problem. They felt that success was very uncertain and that proceeding down such a road would lead Portugal to an untenable position in which it would find itself under attack, with its forces dispersed on four continents.[40] He described the military course of action as chancy, if not suicidal, because of a lack of resources and the ability neither to win on the battlefield nor achieve a favourable political solution to colonial ownership.[41] The pursuit of such a course would generate considerable friction, particularly with the United Kingdom, the United States and Brazil. A change of direction, he argued, was needed to correct the moral injustices in the *ultramar,* and at home and to regain international prestige, something present policies had been unable to achieve. Political freedoms were needed so that Portugal could expand socially and economically.

The uprisings served to highlight the differing opinions. After considerable debate, virtually the entire defence staff decided that a motion of no confidence in Salazar should be made at the approaching Council meeting on 8 April. Salazar, tipped to the plans by Arriaga, did not attend the meeting. As an alternative, the plotters had asked President Américo Tomás to dismiss Salazar. Tomás indicated that he would not dismiss the "greatest statesman of the century after Churchill". By then Salazar had identified the opposition and, on 13 April, in what became known as the *Abrilada* (April revolt), the relevant participants were reassigned or retired. The inevitable reshuffle ensued in which Salazar assumed the defence portfolio, and no change in policy was brooked.

Salazar had managed over the years of his rule to control and manipulate the military through a strategy of co-optation and 'divide and rule'.[42] Military pay was poor, and to advance in pay and promotion, ambitious officers were removed from the immediate military environment through postings to lucrative and prestigious special positions. Normally these were at high levels of government in both the *metrópole* and the *ultramar*, and it was these postings, promotions and pay that Salazar oversaw. Allegiances were ambivalent. This undermining of traditional military bonds enabled Salazar to create mistrust and fear within the armed forces to his advantage. Until the 1974 revolution, when the coup participants had developed broad and determined backing, the Salazar regime would be safe from a military takeover, and despite its enormous reservations and latent moral indignation, the armed forces would be forced to honour his commitment to the colonies and fight his war in Africa.[43] With this event it became evident that the purpose of his colonial policy was now in large part to preserve the Salazar regime. Advocates of any alternate colonial option had been neutralized, and thus the commitment to war had been reinforced through the destruction of the opposition. These events accented the increasing international isolation of Portugal.

UN reversal of 1961

International isolation of Portugal had been growing ever since it had joined the United Nations in 1955 following a number of vetoes by the Soviet Union. Pressure had been building from UN members for Portugal to grant self-rule to its colonies. This

General Botelho Moniz
Photo Arquivo Histórico Militar

Colonel Kaúlza de Arriaga
Photo Arquivo Histórico Militar

Colonel Almeida Fernandes
Photo Arquivo Histórico Militar

Colonel Costa Gomes
Photo Arquivo Histórico Militar

agitation had been fed by the newly independent states joining the United Nations and by the writings of several authors highlighting the human abuses in Portuguese policy toward the colonies, most notably a report by Captain Henrique Galvão. Galvão was the Chief Inspector of the Colonial Administration and his report in 1947 described the labour conditions in Angola and warned against their continuance.[44] Salazar had the report banned and in 1952 arrested Galvão on treason charges. This incident drew unfavourable international attention. Portugal also refused to submit the periodic technical reports on its colonies, as required by the United Nations for non-self-governing territories. While the other colonial powers were unhappy in disclosing facts about their colonies, they complied. Portugal attracted additional negative attention in its refusal.

In 1955 a group of nations advocating colonial independence, with the support of the Soviet Union, orchestrated the passage of a resolution condemning colonialism as a violation of human rights and the UN Charter. In response, Portugal claimed that it had no colonies, as all its overseas provinces were part of a single state with one constitution. It also claimed that the United Nations had no jurisdiction in this matter, as it was an internal affair. The issue was debated for four years and, finally, on 15 December 1960, the UN General Assembly, again pushed by this group and the Soviets, ruled against Portugal. Portugal saw itself as victimized and refused to accept the resolution. The NATO alliance partners closed ranks with Portugal in the face of the United Nations in preventing a catastrophe; however, this support began to fray in 1961.[45] Following the UPA assault, the UN Security Council convened in May and June to discuss the events in Angola. The United States, under President John F. Kennedy, reversed support in this forum and sided with the Soviet Union in condemning Portuguese African policy. This event was an enormous blow to Salazar, who criticized the United States for voting with the Soviet Union in the face of historical opposition. Portugal was thus destined to become a semi-pariah state, politically isolated along with its colonial neighbours, South Africa and Southern Rhodesia, and was forced to fight the ensuing war hobbled by this isolation. It felt beleaguered and viewed its position as neither understood nor appreciated. This ostracism served to cement its commitment

Captain Henrique Galvão
Photo Arquivo Histórico Militar

General António de Spinola
Photo Arquivo Histórico Militar

to its colonies. Portugal believed that it was acting properly and responsibly and had nothing of which to be ashamed. It proceeded accordingly, defending its sovereign territory and interests.

Collapse of Gôa

This beleaguered colonial position was reinforced by the actual loss of Portuguese India in what was an act of war that Portugal was powerless to prevent. The events surrounding Gôa in 1961 again hardened the Portuguese position by providing Salazar with a nationally distressing event to coalesce the population for the coming African conflict. While Portuguese Indian territory was relatively small, at 4,194 square kilometres, its seizure by India was a blatant act of aggression against another sovereign state.

Portugal had three trading enclaves there: Gôa, Damão and Diu.[46] The fledgling Indian government had threatened to take these properties in the late 1940s, as it considered them an affront. The British prime minister, Winston Churchill, along with the United States, forcefully intervened to moderate Indian ambitions. Later, on 27 February 1950, the Indian government presented a formal memorandum stating its position on these possessions and asking that negotiations over their future commence immediately. On 15 June, Portugal responded by rejecting such negotiations but proposed continued discussions to resolve day-to-day problems arising from the contiguousness of the territories and

View of the fort and church of Reis Magos, the sea entrance to Gôa. The fort was built by the Portuguese in 1551, and the church in 1555 on the site of an earlier Hindu temple.
Photo Souza & Paul (Central Library Archives, Gôa)

Governor-General Manuel António Vassalo e Silva (seated centre), negotiating the terms of surrender with Indian Chief of Army Staff, General Pran Thapar (seated right) in Gôa.
Photo Arquivo Histórico Militar

Indian troops invade Gôa. *Photo Arquivo Histórico Militar*

their interdependent economies. This exchange represented an impasse. The issue was again formally addressed on 14 January 1953, but the position of each country remained unaltered. From this point on, relations between the two degenerated progressively.

Prime Minister Jawaharlal Nehru, newly emboldened by the outbreak of armed revolt in Angola, made some very peremptory demands of the Portuguese, a manifestation of the bitter feeling he held against the permanent Portuguese presence on the Malabar Coast.[47] When the Portuguese position was again made clear, India massed 30,000 troops, supported by tanks, aircraft and warships, on the borders of the three territories. Governor-General Manuel António Vassalo e Silva could defend his territory with only around 3,000 ill-equipped troops, 900 Goan police and an old frigate. He had neither air support nor air defence. On 11 December, Salazar attempted to invoke the Anglo-Portuguese Treaty without success. Great Britain had since 1954 refused to help, saying that the 600-year-old alliance had clear limitations, particularly since a member of the Commonwealth was involved. New alliance structures, such as NATO, had clearly replaced the Anglo-Portuguese Treaty in both intent and practice.

Salazar gave instructions that resistance must last at least eight days to mobilize international support. Should that not be forthcoming, then 'total sacrifice' must be made to save Portuguese honour. Indian forces invaded in the morning of 17 December in a blitzkrieg that frustrated Salazar's intentions, and Vassalo e Silva capitulated in the pointless struggle on 19 December, far short of eight days and total sacrifice.[48] Vassalo e Silva and the other officers involved were dismissed from the army in 1963 in what appeared to be an effort to shift blame for the loss of Portuguese India to the military and to set an example for officers in similar situations, such as the colonial wars. The military at large was resentful at the unjust punishment and in making soldiers the scapegoats for poor national policy. The armed forces carried into the African campaigns this "ominous message that the government was prepared to manipulate and sacrifice them in hopeless missions and to court-martial virtually all survivors".[49] General António de Spínola, who was to be the Commander-in-Chief of Portuguese forces in Guiné (1968–72), the Deputy Chief of the General Staff (1972–74), and the first president of the new government following the revolution in 1974, described in his controversial book, *Portugal and the Future,* the anxiety permeating the entire Portuguese military on the eve of the African wars: "India is a clear example of what we fear. Never was its inevitable loss believed possible. And yet when the tragedy happened, the Nation's attention was immediately focused on the narrow aspect of military conduct. The Armed Forces were accused of not having defended India heroically; when, in reality, no matter how effective its defence, India would have fallen in only a matter of days."[50]

The punishment for the leaders of the Indian garrison carried the broad message that there would be no turning back from Salazar's decision to defend the colonies. His commitment to preserving his regime was unswerving in its purpose, and the events in Gôa served to push Portugal farther down the road to war.

Political opposition to Salazar was tolerated neither at home nor in the *ultramar.* The long-standing abuses of Portuguese African populations thus created widespread dissatisfaction with no outlet. Between the intransigent Salazar and an aggrieved African population an explosion was inevitable. When it happened in 1961, the events in Angola, along with the *Abrilada*, the isolation in the United Nations and the seizing of Gôa pushed Salazar to solidify the commitment of Portugal to defend its colonies and hence preserve his regime. This national commitment was a reflection of his own personal determination and his propensity to brook no opposition, particularly from seemingly upstart nationalist movements and elements of his military. So strong was this feeling that it defied any voice of reason and foreclosed any retreat or compromise over African affairs. Ignoring the element of chance in war and Clausewitz's caution that the most far-reaching act of judgment for a statesman and commander is to understand the kind of war on which he is embarking, Salazar pledged the armed forces and treasure of Portugal in full as the ultimate manifestation of his intent to make the colonial system work according to his concept of empire.[51]

1   William C. Atkinson, 'Introduction' to Luís Vaz de Camões, *The Lusiads*, trans. William C. Atkinson (Harmondsworth: Penguin Books, 1952), pp. 19-20. King Sebastião's force totalled some 15,000 foot and 1,500 horse with 9,000 camp followers. Five hundred vessels were required to transport the force. Eight thousand were killed, 15,000 were taken prisoner and sold into slavery and perhaps 100 eventually reached the safety of Portugal.

2   Marcello Caetano, ;Editorial', *O Mundo Português* [Portuguese World], 2 (1935): p. 218.

3   *O Brado Africano* (Lourenço Marques), 27 February 1931.

4   John A. Marcum, *The Angolan Revolution, Vol. I, The Anatomy of an Explosion (1950–1962)* (Cambridge: MIT Press, 1969), pp. 347-51. Marcum lists some 59 groups affecting Angola alone beginning in the 1940s and either merging with one another or vanishing by 1962.

5   Malyn Newitt, *Portugal in Africa: The Last Hundred Years* (London: C. Hurst & Co., 1981), p. 190.

6   Douglas L. Wheeler & René Pélissier, *Angola* (London: Pall Mall Press, 1971), p. 167. The authors cite as an example the Congo district in 1960. For its 37,000 square miles, it had 14 *concelhos* (basic urban or semi-urban administrative unit) or *circunscrições* (basic rural administrative division) and 37 posts, for an average of 725 square miles per administrative division. This presence would hardly be effective in controlling a frontier, as the posts would be dozens of miles apart. Large numbers of people could and did cross undetected.

7   Hélio Felgas, *Angola e a Evolução Política dos Territórios Vizinhos* [Angola and the Political Evolution of the Neighboring Territories], Revista Militar (December 1965): p. 706.

8   Shola Adenekan, 'Holden Roberto', *The New Black Magazine*, 22 October 2007, http://www.thenewblackmagazine.com/view.aspx?index=1042 (accessed 23 March 2009).

9   Ibid.

10 Willem S. van der Waals, *Portugal's War in Angola, 1961–1974* (Rivonia: Ashanti Publishing, 1993), pp. 96-7. The author argues that Portuguese propaganda and social work among the refugees in Angola persuaded most of these displaced people to move into controlled settlements. This development deprived ELNA of popular support. ELNA had concentrated on military action in a human desert and on preventing MPLA infiltration. It had neglected to indoctrinate, organize or win recruits among refugees returning to Angola, and thus missed an opportunity to undermine Portuguese authority. Consequently, no ELNA internal political infrastructure was established in Angola. Portugal gained the upper hand and maintained superior momentum until 1974.

11 René Pélissier, *La Colonie du Minotaure, Nationalismes et Révoltes en Angola (1926–1961)* [The Colony of the Minotaur, Nationalist Movements and Revolts in Angola (1926–1961)] (Orgeval: Editions Pélissier, 1978), p. 658.

12 Alex Vines, 'Holden Roberto', *The Independent* (London), 8 August 2007, http://www.independent.co.uk/news/obituaries/holden-roberto-460658.hmtl (accessed 23 March 2009).

13 van der Waals, p. 96.

14 Neil Bruce, 'Portugal's African Wars', *Conflict Studies* 34 (March 1973), p. 22.

15 Sue Armstrong, *In Search of Freedom* (Gibraltar: Ashanti Publishing, 1989), p. 71.

16 Adenekan.

17 Ibid.

18 Piero Gleijeses, *Conflicting Missions: Havana, Washington, and Africa, 1959–1976* (Chapel Hill: University of North Carolina Press, 2002), p. 239.

19 *Expresso* (Lisbon), 17 September 1974, p. 18.

20 Gleijeses, p. 238.

21 Alex Vines, 'Holden Roberto', *The Independent* (London), 8 August 2007, http://www.independent.co.uk/news/obituaries/holden-roberto-460658.hmtl (accessed 23 March 2009).

22 Ibid. Mobutu renamed the Congo in 1971 as Zaïre.

23 Adenekan.

24 Gleijeses, p. 238.

25 Ibid, p. 295.

26 Patrick Chabal, *Amílcar Cabral* (Cambridge: Cambridge University Press, 1983), pp. 56-7.

27 Imigrantes Somos Todas, 'Moçambique: A Guerra de Liberação (1964–1974)' [Mozambique: The War of Liberation (1964–1974)]: http://imigrantes.no.sapo.pt/page2mocGLibert.html (accessed 4 February 2010).

28 Eduardo Mondlane, *The Struggle for Mozambique* (London: Zed Press, 1969), p. 125.

29 Gerald J. Bender, 'The Limits of Counterinsurgency: An African Case', *Comparative Politics*, 4, no. 3 (April 1972), p. 357.

30 Douglas L. Wheeler, 'The Portuguese Army in Angola', *Modern African Studies*, 7, no. 3 (October 1969), p. 430.

31 Douglas L. Wheeler, 'African Elements in Portugal's Armies in Africa (1961–1974)', *Armed Forces and Society* 2, No. 2 (February 1976), p. 237.

32 Estado-Maior do Exército, *Resenha Histórico-Militar das Campanhas de África, Vol. II, Dispositivo das Nossas Forças Angola* [Historical-Military Report on the African Campaigns, Vol. II, Disposition of Our Angolan Forces] (Lisbon: Estado-Maior do Exército, 1989), pp. 63-5.

33 Douglas L. Wheeler, 'The Portuguese Army in Angola', *Modern African Studies*, 7, no. 3 (October 1969), p. 431.

34 Alex Vines.

35 Charles Burke Elbrick, U.S. Ambassador to Portugal, Lisbon, Telegram 508 to U.S. Secretary of State, Washington, 18 February 1961.

36 Ibid.

37 W. Gervase Clarence-Smith, *The Third Portuguese Empire 1825–1975: A Study in Economic Imperialism* (Manchester: Manchester University Press, 1985), p. 193. The author argues that by 1968 the Portuguese economy was turning decisively from the colonies toward Europe. Portugal in the course of the 1960s and early 1970s became a booming and aggressive "newly industrialized country" and was described as a "Taiwan of southern Europe".

38 António de Spínola, *País sem Rumo* [Country without Direction] (Lisbon: Editorial SCIRE, 1978), p. 83.

39 Douglas Porch, *The Portuguese Armed Forces and the Revolution* (Stanford: The Hoover Institution Press, 1977), p. 38.

40 José Krus Abecasis, *Bordo de Ataque, Memórias de uma Caderneta de Voo e um Contributo para a História* [Attack Heading, Memories from an Aviation Log Book and a Contribution to History] (Coimbra: Coimbra Editora, 1985), pp. 245-8.

41 Sérgio Augusto Margarido Lima Bacelar, *A Guerra em* África *1961–1974: Estratégias Adoptadas pelas Forças Armadas* [The War in Africa 1961–1974: Strategies Adopted by the Armed Forces] (Porto: Liga dos Amigos do Museu Militar do Porto & Universidade Portucalense Infante D. Henrique, 2000), p. 39.

42 Douglas L. Wheeler, 'The Military and the Portuguese Dictatorship, 1926–1974: "The Honor of the Army"', in *Contemporary Portugal*, ed. Lawrence S. Graham & Harry M. Makler (Austin: University of Texas Press, 1979), p. 199.

43 Porch, p. 26.

44 Captain Henrique Galvão, *Report on Native Problems in the Portuguese Colonies* (Lisbon: Ministry of the Colonies, 1947).

45 Joaquim Moreira da Silva Cunha, *O Ultramar, a Nação e o '25 de Abril'* [The Overseas Provinces, the Nation and the '25th of April'] (Coimbra: Atlântida Editora, 1977), pp. 13-14.

46 The actual Portuguese possessions within the peninsula are Gôa, Damão and Diu. Gôa is a tract of picturesque and fertile country on the West Coast about 250 miles south of Bombay, measuring 63 miles in length by 40 miles in breadth. It comprises a nucleus of 'old conquests', Gôa, Bardez and Salcete, an outer belt of 'new conquests', and the island of Angediva. The population borders on half a million, the majority of whom are native Catholics whose ancestors were converted centuries ago. Damão, 100 miles north of Bombay, a fortified Portuguese town with a small outlying district in the interior, has an area of 82 square miles with a total population of over 50,000. Diu is a small fortified island at the southern point of the Kathiawar coast, measuring about

seven miles by two, with a population of something over 12,000.

47 Richard Robinson, *Contemporary Portugal* (London: George Allen & Unwin, 1979), p. 103; and Krus Abecasis, p. 259. Nehru announced that India was "not prepared to tolerate the presence of the Portuguese in Gôa, even if the Goans want them to be there".

48 Actually, not all Portuguese felt that the loss of Gôa was a catastrophe. Father John Paul, an Anglican missionary in Mozambique, writes, "One of my more enlightened friends in Vila Cabral said, however, that he thought it quite a good thing Portugal had been forced to abandon Gôa, since the millions of escudos that had been poured into the place to keep it going for the sake of Portugal's prestige could now be diverted to the more worthy cause of developing Portugal and her overseas territories in Africa." See John Paul,

Mozambique, Memoirs of a Revolution (Harmondsworth: Penguin Books, 1975), p. 87.

49 Porch, p. 36.

50 António de Spínola, *Portugal e o Futuro* [Portugal and the Future] (Lisbon: Editoria Arcádia, 1974), p. 235.

51 Carl von Clausewitz, *On War*, ed. and trans. Michael Howard & Peter Paret (Princeton: Princeton University Press, 1976), p. 88. The actual quotation is, "The first, the supreme, the most far-reaching act of judgement that the statesman and commander have to make is to establish by that test the kind of war on which they are embarking; neither mistaking it for, nor trying to turn it into, something that is alien to its nature."

CHAPTER TWO:
LEARNING COUNTERINSURGENCY

Following the 15 March attacks, Portugal sought to deploy its forces as rapidly as possible to Angola. While some troops were airlifted, such as the paratroops, the majority came from the *metrópole* by sea. Between the months of May and December 1961, troop strength was augmented from 6,500 to 33,477.[1] These troops landed in Luanda and, as they became available over this eight-month period, moved to subdue the UPA/FNLA threat and regain control in the north of the territory. The transition from a small force, aimed at reaction and defence to a large one of reoccupation and neutralization, was gradual, as it was dependent on transportation resources that were not designed for military power projection.

There were also problems in troop competence in these new arrivals. While counterinsurgency by its nature requires substantial numbers of light infantry, the force must be trained in the craft of fighting a 'small war' to be effective. The majority of the arriving troops had no such indoctrination and had been readied at an accelerated pace, including uniforms. Indicative of the rush, Portugal had only a limited inventory of colonial uniforms for its troops at the time and had to hastily craft a washed khaki wardrobe. These uniforms became known as 'canaries' because of their yellow hue. They were not ideally suited to fighting in the bush, and, as a more considered design in camouflage became available, the canaries went to the back of the closet. There would be many more substantial examples of adjusting, and these would occur largely in shaping the approach to counterinsurgency. In reoccupying the north and addressing the UPA/FNLA threat, Portugal quickly realized that its most effective forces were those with special qualifications. Initially these were the light infantry called 'special hunters', who had advanced training. There were

Portuguese troops entering Luanda wearing their new 'canary' uniforms. *Photo Arquivo Histórico Militar*

The 4th CCE on a trail in the bush, northern Angola, 1961. *Photo Archive www.4cce.org with kind permission*

also very small numbers of elite forces. These were the air force paratroops, the navy *fuzileiros*, or marines, and the aforementioned army 'special hunter' infantry companies, although the latter had neither the rigorous selection process nor the elevated training of the first two. The maturing experiences of Portuguese forces and their consequent adjustments to fight a counterinsurgency led to development of specialized, tailored units to close the gaps in skills and knowledge between the insurgents and Portuguese forces.

Special forces development

Initially, the post-World War II Portuguese army seemed to have had mixed emotions about the need for elite, special-purpose forces that operated in small units with the attendant flexibility and elevated lethality. 'Shock troops' have been traditionally controversial, as even the vaunted military theorist Baron Carl von Clausewitz saw little point to them. This attitude affected most modern general staff officers, regardless of nationality, and almost certainly encouraged their general opposition to irregular forces and unorthodox forms of warfare. The history of the paratroops in the Portuguese army and their eventual home in the enlightened Portuguese air force in 1955 is illustrative of this ambivalent view. Nevertheless, in a war of the weak in which insurgents avoid government strengths and exploit its weaknesses using agility, deception and imagination, such small, crack government units are particularly well-suited to counterinsurgency operations. This appreciation emerged with the evolution of the war.

As early as April 1959, the army established its Centre of Instruction for Special Operations (*Centro de Instrução de Operações*

Especiais or CIOE) in the *metrópole* and formed a battalion of four companies from volunteers as its initial class. The instruction emphasized the techniques of combat and the psychological preparation for battle. The psychological component was perhaps the most important and distinctive to the training, as its objective was to transform the recruit into a disciplined, competent and confident soldier who would be able to adjust to all circumstances and fight effectively. The training was marked by a high degree of realism and the endless execution of procedural drills to make fighting second nature to the soldier. By September 1959, the initial three companies of the battalion had been formed and by April 1960 were graduated. The final Company of Special Hunters (*Companhia de Caçadores Especiais* or CCE) followed two months later in June, and all four were deployed to Angola that month. They wore the new brown beret and the first camouflage uniforms ever issued by the Portuguese army. It now appeared that Portugal was changing its army to fit the approaching war rather than trying to change the war to fit its army, as these new troops were trained for and adapted to the environment in which they were expected to fight. While an important first step, 480 troops with advanced infantry training were not enough to make a difference in the crisis of northern Angola.

As the war progressed, particularly the reoccupation of the north, the urgent need for additional specially trained troops became clear, that is those troops whose training went well beyond the traditional instruction and even beyond that of the CCEs. Such troops would be formed into units capable of operating independently for extended periods in the field. This need came to the fore during the employment in early 1962 of an infantry battalion to the vicinity of Nóqui, a frontier port on the Congo River. Accompanying the battalion was an Italian journalist, Cesare Dante Vacchi, who held a wealth of combat experience from both Indochina and Algeria and wrote for *Paris Match*. He befriended the officers and men of the battalion, and, as he learned their language, began to offer instruction based not only in the technical tradecraft of soldering but also, and more importantly, in the psychological preparation that enabled the troops to acclimate quickly to the confusion of combat. As the strong results of Vacchi's coaching became widely apparent, it was felt that this more sophisticated and advanced preparation should be the basis of a specialized body of highly capable troops. Consequently, in late 1962, after extensive briefings of key generals, Colonel José Bettencourt Rodrigues, the Chief of Staff of the Military Region, was given a free hand in establishing the new units and their training centre at Zemba, a site about 80 miles northeast of Luanda. In 1963, the first of these new troops, called commandos, were deployed in small numbers and organized in platoon-sized commando groups (*grupos de comandos*). In September 1964, the 1st Company of Commandos began operations from Belo Horizonte, the new commando base located in the north of Angola. These commandos also proudly wore the new, distinctive crimson beret.

Overseeing all this was Lieutenant-Colonel Gilberto Manuel Santos e Castro, under whose tutelage commando instructors took great pains to stay abreast of the latest enemy operational methods and to maintain the 'warrior edge' in their training. This edge, in essence, was an approach to fighting that continually pushed the commandos to think of themselves as the hunter rather than the hunted. Officers returning from contact with the enemy were rigorously debriefed, and commando instructors regularly participated in operations to learn of the latest enemy developments. This information was integrated with intelligence from other sources gathered by the military and national intelligence services, and from such training was constantly revised to stay attuned to the enemy and his behaviour. The commandos became a breed apart and their reputation was such that when insurgents discovered a unit deployed in their area, they would generally withdraw until the killers left. This commando training and its sympathy with the fighting environment foreshadowed the development and use of additional special troops for tasks peculiar to local physical, cultural and geopolitical environments. The Flechas would become just such specifically formed troops.

A changing enemy

The UPA/FNLA was changing too, as the conflict had shifted from fluid chaos into an organized insurgency. By mid-May 1961, it controlled an enormous area in the north of Angola, an estimated 7,200 square miles.[2] Further, some 48 villages had been abandoned by the population. Since the March attacks, the UPA/FNLA had continuously received instruction in fighting techniques and material aid in the form of modern weapons from abroad, and this external support began to alter the face of the

Gilberto Santos e Castro
Photo Personal archive of Coronel Raúl Folques

conflict. The *canhangulos*, primitive firearms made with water pipes stolen from farms, were exchanged for automatic rifles. The frontal attacks were replaced with the refinement of ambushes, each more carefully planned. Mines began to appear on the main unpaved roads and their dirt trail access routes.

In early January 1962, two scholars of Portuguese Africa, George Houser and John Marcum, were hosted by the UPA/FNLA on a tour of the north. During their two-week stay, they walked more than 200 miles over an "interwoven network of trails leading through forests and elephant grass, across vine and single-log bridges, and around open-pit animal traps to the hidden semiportable villages that constituted nationalist Angola".[3] Marcum's description of UPA/FNLA organization reflects a hierarchical one in which orders, arms, ammunition, medicines and other supplies were delivered from the Congo and found their way south to hidden camps over an intricate and constantly shifting system of footpaths.[4] These secret paths were important in avoiding detection by Portuguese security forces. They originated in the Congo, crossed the border and wound their way as far south as Úcua, some 150 miles from the frontier and 70 miles east of Luanda.[5] The coordinating centre for these lines of communication was an encampment known as Fuessi (Portuguese) or Fuesse (French), which was located about halfway between the frontier posts of Luvo and Buela and overseen by the UPA/FNLA functionary Frederico Deves.[6] From here the trails led south, some 50 miles to an operational headquarters near Bembe. Here the UPA/FNLA operational commander, João Batista, received desperately needed weapons and munitions and rationed them to the 40-odd military sectors whose representatives gathered periodically to receive their quotas.[7] The weapons came from various sources within the Congo, where several sympathetic nations had forces under a UN peacekeeping operation. Supplies to these forces did not receive proper oversight,

Bailundo workers clearing a roadway in the north of Angola, April 1961. *Photo Horácio Caio*

A pit in a Dembos road designed to stop a column for ambush. Note the improvised armour plating attached to the Land Rovers for personnel protection. *Photo Horácio Caio*

and fulfilling other menial tasks around its encampments.[12] For the insurgents operating in Angola, local knowledge was a critical vulnerability, as they were invariably dependent on the population for this resource.

Marcum describes an area apocryphally controlled by the UPA/FNLA, reaching from the northern border roughly 200 miles into Angola and extending 150 miles in breadth.[13] Within this zone the UPA/FNLA had ostensibly established a rudimentary system of self-government. Ideally everyone travelled with an identity card issued by the UPA/FNLA in Léopoldville, and this card was checked frequently, as people travelled the paths and often crossed between one of the 50 UPA/FNLA 'administrative districts'.[14] The headquarters for these districts lay in settlements similar to Fuessi, where there were elective councils, youth groups, a dispensary and a school teacher with a few tattered books.[15] Supposedly days began in these encampments with mass prayers and patriotic ceremonies. These were punctuated with a motivational talk from the local UPA/FNLA leader, perhaps Batista.[16] For the UPA/FNLA, the reversal in the field began in January 1962, about the time of Houser's and Marcum's visit, and occurred following Portuguese reoccupation of the significant commercial and population centres in the north. Once this was accomplished, security forces began to move outward from these centres and pacify the surrounding countryside in an 'oil spot' strategy. The primary impediment was the forbidding environment, and this too would have to be conquered.

Key events in this advance on the centres included the ground reoccupation in July of Nambuangongo, or 'Nambu' as the troops called it, and the air assaults on Quipedro in early August, Serra de Canda in late August and Sacandia in September. Large-scale operations to reopen the lines of communication were difficult and slow, as when the offensive to retake the north began in May of 1961, the columns were constantly forced to halt to clear trees felled across the roads, repair bridges destroyed right down to the foundation piers and fill pits and trenches in the centre of the roadways. The scope of the problem was enormous and, as an example, the Baptist missionary David Grenfell noted that between Bungu and 31 de Janeiro, a stretch of about 18 miles, the road was blocked by 800 trees and 200 trenches.[17]

Advancing road-bound troops constantly found themselves in classic ambush scenarios and frequently took intense fire from UPA/FNLA gunmen hiding in the thick, tall grass 15 to 20 feet

and such purposeful laxness enabled arms to be moved through the sympathetic supply chains to the UPA/FNLA. According to Marcum, the "nationalist patrols hoisted their loads into woven palm leaves" and trekked for two to three weeks into the interior.[8] Yet the reality was that the UPA/FNLA leaders, who had spent most of their lives in the Belgian Congo and were thus foreign to Angola, depended on local headmen to furnish them with porters and guides to move these supplies and munitions overland in the needed volume.[9] This dependence reinforced local patterns of leadership, as the UPA/FNLA could not ignore the indigenous authorities when depending on their assistance.[10] Interestingly, the dependence on guides raised the status of local hunter-gatherers whose knowledge of the immediate terrain made them invaluable. It was not easy to find reliable porters and guides, and often UPA/FNLA goods and people were immobilized because no one with this critical local knowledge was available.[11] Those with such skills held a certain leverage over the UPA/FNLA and could count on decent treatment, for the UPA/FNLA had a practice of punishing those without a proper identity card (*guia*) by forcing them to perform what was essentially slave labour in maintaining the trails high that grew to the immediate edge of the road. It was precisely as the men left the vehicles and were most vulnerable that the rebels attacked. This skilful setting of ambushes and the creation of killing zones were new refinements that clearly came from outside the UPA/FNLA. Likewise, ambushes increasingly made good use of the terrain, another newly imported skill, and during these attacks it was noted that the UPA/FNLA wore a quasi-uniform of blue trousers with white or red bands on them.[18]

Road vs. bush

There was initially an irrational fear of the unfamiliar bush by the Portuguese troops. Bush terrain could vary, but most often it was tall, thick elephant grass that extended to the immediate margin of the roadway. If the roads were not used often, then

Sergeant Lúcio of Battalion 96 raises the national flag from the church roof in the ruined town of Nambuangongo on 9 August 1961.
Photo Arquivo Histórico Militar

The 4th CCE advances along a trail in northern Angola, 1961 closely bordered by elephant grass, an ideal environment for enemy ambush.
Photo Archive www.4cce.org with kind permission

the bush would encroach, and passage would require trimming back the new growth. The bush concealed insurgents, refugees, citizens who wished to be ignored by the authorities, dangerous animals and often more. The bush itself contained a network of trails devoted to each of these users and represented a native community as opposed to the road network connecting centres of commerce dominated by the 'civilized' Europeans. These two communities and their very different environments were in constant tension, and in order to find and destroy the enemy effectively, the Portuguese were forced to address this foreign medium successfully.

The roads used by the Portuguese were seen by the UPA/FNLA as an impediment to its insurgency, for they brought Portuguese troops to the area. Crossing them was always chancy, even for the small mobile groups of ten to 12 men suited to hit-and-run action.[19] Their tracks would be left in the dirt surface, and these would potentially provide clues for the Portuguese patrols pursuing them. Insurgents and refugees alike crossed only with great caution and chose stony areas so as not to leave traces. Indeed, often great detours were made to avoid crossing a road. Formal roadways were thus not only a means of transportation for the Portuguese but also a quasi-weapon, as a road meant a form of victory over the bush, the habitat of the insurgent.[20] The Portuguese realized this in Angola and undertook one of the most impressive road-building programmes in Africa

With the ostensible goals of aiding economic expansion, supporting military operations and connecting the district capitals, the Portuguese bent to road construction with a relentless will. At the beginning of the war, Angola had about 21,727 miles of road; in 1974 that figure exceeded 48,000, with 12 per cent asphalted, 38 per cent tarred with gravel or dirt surfaces and 50 per cent rough dirt tracks that were generally impassable in the rainy season.[21] This dramatic effort was made even more impressive by the difficult terrain that the Portuguese often encountered. Colonel Souza at the Eastern Intervention Zone headquarters in Luso described some of these difficulties in a 1968 interview with the journalist Al Venter: "Almost the entire region was overlaid with sand up to a depth of about five metres. In some areas the sand went down to more than 40 metres. It is impossible to build roads on this kind of foundation. We do, of course, have some good roads, but it's a giant task keeping them serviceable."[22]

This construction also entailed a major bridging effort. The military began upgrading the road system in June 1960 and completed its work by mid-1964. It took ten battalions of engineers 50 months, at the rate of 90,000 man-hours per 60 miles of road to build, repair or maintain the system.[23] Building of new roads continued under private paving contractors until 1974 at the rate of about 660 miles a year.

Conversely, the bush constantly threatened the road, as the vegetation persistently encroached. Initially the bush was *terra incognita* to Portuguese troops, and the UPA/FNLA sought to take advantage of this ignorance and fear by establishing secret routes through it for their lines of communication. Within the forests

Road construction in Angola. *Photo Fernando Farinha*

their traditional habits and to be on a road or in a town but not in the bush. This habitually belonged to the local people, at least in their way of thinking, and the Portuguese disrupted this relationship in appropriating the trails. This reversed the hunter–hunted relationship, and as much as the UPA/FNLA, and later the MPLA, tried, neither insurgent organization could undo this newly structured hierarchy. This shift was not an easy development, and certainly not a uniform one, as Portuguese troops generally viewed the bush with unease, almost verging on irrational fear. To them it was the source of danger from a sheltered enemy. It took confidence and understanding of the foreign, unfamiliar bush for a Portuguese soldier to enter it in search of the enemy. Ultimately his anxiety and fear were conquered through the use of natives who knew how to read its signs and survive in it and taught him these skills. Use of such troops, particularly in a supporting role with other special troops, was to prove devastating to the enemy over the long haul. This drawing on local skills in support of regular forces would lead to the establishment of the Flechas.

and elephant grass there were numerous trails specific to the user. According to the scholar Inge Brinkman, there were at least five types:

- Animal trails
- Insurgent paths
- Refugee paths
- Local paths for residents living in a particular section of the bush
- Cross-border paths that secretly crossed the frontier between Angola and the Congo.[24]

The animal trails were to be avoided by humans, as they were infested by insects and could be otherwise dangerous. The incoming insurgent trails were to be avoided by refugees, as no army wants refugees clogging its routes.[25] Also, because clearing and maintenance of the insurgent routes were generally performed by impressed labour, refugees sought to avoid this entrapment.

Gradually the Portuguese began to understand the existence and importance of these bush paths, and started watching them to gather intelligence, establish ambushes and lay anti-personnel mines. They also created settlements along them to disrupt insurgent logistics.[26] As pacification progressed, Portuguese forces were able to encircle and isolate UPA/FNLA strongholds in the bush and thereby reduce their utility. By the end of 1961, many of these clandestine routes had been discovered by Portuguese forces and their use became risky. In reaction, UPA/FNLA insurgents, once ambushed on a particular trail, would never again use it.[27]

Brinkman describes a "moral geography" that the Portuguese disturbed on entering the bush.[28] They were expected to follow

Fuessi

An excellent example of struggling with the unfamiliar bush was the assault on Fuessi. As the Portuguese began to identify and reduce the UPA/FNLA strongholds, air power played an increasingly important role. From the UPA/FNLA standpoint, the air force was making more effective use of its resources with its armed reconnaissance and localized destruction missions.[29] The UPA/FNLA countered with slit trenches as air raid shelters, mock villages as decoy targets and a warning system of spotters. Nevertheless, according to Marcum, the air raids were devastating.[30] Another setback was Batista's death. He was killed in an ill-conceived UPA/FNLA raid on a Portuguese camp at Bembe that had, unbeknown to him, been recently reinforced. His outnumbered force was destroyed in a counterattack on 6 February, a month following Marcum's visit.[31] The next blow came at Fuessi.

Portuguese intelligence had identified the dangerous settlement and headquarters, from where mobile groups were regularly laying ambushes throughout the area, and sought to destroy the centre and its ability to make mischief.[32] On 20 April 1962, the 1st Company of the elite Parachute Battalion 21 was airlifted from

Luanda to São Sālvador and began its march on Fuessi. The objective was about 18 miles east of Luvo in an area of difficult access. The only approach was by a footpath that had not been travelled in a year and was thought to be abandoned. The company of 120 men travelled by truck from São Salvador to Mamarrosa and after that followed a road until reaching the River Lunguege. Here the troops left the trucks, forded the river and proceeded on foot, as the bridge had been destroyed, and the vehicles could not continue. The rough track leading away from the bridge degenerated into a path that was overgrown and difficult to follow. It was also crossed by other trails and the route became very confusing. The guide, Pedro Tumissongo, was familiar with the routes around Luvo and south thereof, but the company had left the area that he knew, and it now depended on a small Dornier observation aircraft from Negage to provide orientation and to drop supplies, as the troops only carried light packs for mobility.[33] This help and the size of the force would have made enough of a disturbance to destroy any element of surprise, as UPA/ FNLA lookouts and sentries

Makeshift bridge crossing the Magina River. *Photo Personal archive of Mário Mendes*

Air drop over abandoned UPA/FNLA headquarters, Fuessi, April 1962. *Photo Força Aérea Portuguesa*

could hear and see the aircraft and detect the approaching column. It was the rainy season and the heat and humidity made going difficult, even with light loads. The progress was further impeded by the need to guard against ambushes, although it was likely that the presence of the Dornier caused the insurgents to retire. Still, there were four additional rivers and miles of bush to cross before arriving at Fuessi, and the pace was laboured. A forewarned enemy would clearly have ample time to react.

The company reached the rivers Maza-Matende, Cai and Magina and forded them before finally reaching the Luvo, which was wide and swollen by the rains with a swift, powerful current.

It took time to rig a line and to cross carefully, one by one, but the passage was done without incident, and the march resumed at an accelerated pace. The company reached Fuessi at noon and deployed quietly, encircling the compound and establishing a counter-ambush formation. Even so, UPA/FNLA lookouts would have been alerted by the Dornier and the approaching paratroops. When the paratroops entered the compound it was deserted, but it was obvious that there had been a large number of people there earlier, as indicated by warm fires, food, plates, utensils and other recently abandoned property. In the living huts there were even photographs of 'mademoiselles' with inscriptions written across them in French and local idioms.[34] In the largest hut, which housed the UPA/FNLA leaders, there was a notice posted on an exterior wall. Pedro Tumissongo read it for the paratroops: "It is possible to enter into this place but difficult to leave; blacks who enter into this place must obey, thereafter, the orders of Holden Roberto."[35] The disappointment of a failed attack was extreme, but then this failure held lessons that would lead to more effective operations. Guides would become more competent, force sizes reduced and power projection more comfortable with the bush. Dorniers alerting the enemy would become a thing of the past.

Quivitas and CMIG-Zero

Dislodging and ridding the north of UPA/FNLA insurgents took much time and patience and was never permanent because of the difficult terrain and remoteness. In the Dembos region and the mountain ranges between Uíge and Quitexe with their dense vegetation, there persisted relatively secure hideouts for the rebels, as described by Houser and Marcum.[36] The Serra do Uíge range was an estimated 36 miles long by three miles wide, and with its mountainous forests represented a true challenge for any ground force assault. Troops crawling through the undulating jungle had to operate in the gloomy shadow of great mossy trees supporting a dark green canopy. The humidity and a web of hanging vines made progress exhausting, and it was easy to become disoriented in this suffocating environment. On two prominent, nearly impregnable summits rising from this torrid landscape was a pair of strong UPA/FNLA redoubts that had survived a string of earlier operations. The first was called Quivitas by the local people, and the second was known by its acronym CMIG-Zero, which stood for the Military Centre for Instruction in Guerrilla Warfare, Number Zero (Centre Militaire d'Instruction Guerrilla–Zero). The latter boasted a parade ground, an elaborate infrastructure of huts and the signature flagpole. Both enjoyed large, open, sweeping approaches and were ably defended by heavy machine guns so positioned to defeat even the most determined assault. Various unsuccessful attempts had been made to destroy these centres since their discovery, but they had had limited effect in reducing enemy capabilities in the area.

In September 1965, the army sector commander allied with the air force to construct a campaign designed to eliminate these two sites permanently. The plan called for a concentrated and lengthy artillery and air bombardment prior to a ground assault. For 20 days artillery and air sorties pounded the installations. From Luanda a steady stream of attack aircraft dropped their ordnance loads on the UPA/FNLA centres. The bombing was so intense that during this period the magazine in Luanda was reduced to a mere two days' supply of munitions.[37] The Luanda offense was supplemented by the 16 lighter but no less lethal attack aircraft from nearby Negage, a mere 20-minute flight away. These light attack aircraft would fly three consecutive sorties without refuelling. On the two return landings, they were rearmed by the ground crews in a few minutes, with their engines still turning before being launched again for further strikes on their targets.[38]

Following the air and artillery offensive, several combat groups of paratroops and other infantry forces were inserted into the mountains and penetrated the redoubts, encountering little enemy resistance. They remained bivouacked on the two mountain summits after the action to ensure that they were not reoccupied, while the enemy fled the Uíge range. Later, at Quivitas, a short runaway was built that simplified logistic support and a permanence of the Portuguese garrison. For the moment, the UPA/FNLA were driven from the north with the exception of some small, isolated pockets so deep in hiding as to be irrelevant.

This was a noisy and expensive operation and far from low key. It was a conventional force-on-force encounter and not counterinsurgency. The insurgents lived to fight another day and had simply given ground in the encounter. Portuguese strategy would shift to target enemy lines of communication and to track and destroy infiltrators before they could become effectively organized. It would also reinforce these efforts with population support.

New fronts

With the general neutralization of these strongholds, the UPA/FNLA and the less active MPLA began to look elsewhere for potential for success. The first new front attempted by both was Cabinda. Next, intelligence pointed to enemy infiltration in the northeast and east of Angola, and detachments were deployed to Malange to conduct reconnaissance missions in the districts of Lunda and Moxico, both vast and inhospitable areas.[39]

By the mid-1960s, neither the UPA/FNLA nor the MPLA had met with any substantial success in a classic subversion of the population in the north or in truly displacing the Portuguese position there. This lack of insurgent progress occurred for several reasons. While the army lacked the manpower and mobility to seal the land border completely in an area of poor roads, dissent between the MPLA and the UPA/FNLA, Léopoldville's favouritism of the UPA/FNLA and Holden Roberto's failure of leadership, all served to limit any insurgent offensive.

Friction between the two movements had its origins in the external recognition and choice of which one was to be the representative government of any independent Angola. As the UPA/FNLA was comprised largely of Bakongo, a people prevalent in the north of Angola and that area of the Congo immediately north of the common border, it felt that it more accurately represented the population of Angola at large, and this view was backed by Léopoldville. However, the MPLA saw things differently and described the tribally based UPA/FNLA as "racist" and "foreign": racist because it was Bakongo-based and foreign because its leadership had no ties with Angola, and the movement could only survive with Mobutu's support.[40] The MPLA on the other hand was comprised largely of the mestiço elite and was perceived to have less in common with its host and the people of Angola. As a consequence, there was competition and open friction between the two, and this misdirected energy diluted the attention of both in prosecuting the insurgency. Indeed, UPA/

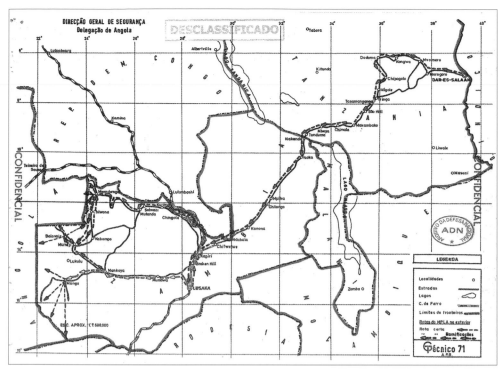

Above: Agostinho Neto

Left: Insurgent infiltration route across Tanzania and Zambia, providing access to eastern Angola from 1968 onward.
Photo Arquivo da Defesa Nacional

FNLA troops took to ambushing MPLA troops in northern Angola, and Portuguese forces often came upon the remnants of these bloody fratricidal scenes.[41]

Léopoldville's favouritism of the UPA/FNLA was unabashed, and it worked to give its chosen movement every advantage. As an example, because of its own security problems, Léopoldville did not permit insurgents to bear arms within its borders. Both the MPLA and UPA/FNLA insurgents would be transported by Congolese soldiers to the Angolan border, where they would be issued their weapons from depositories. On returning from operations, their weapons would be cantoned, and they would return to their training base with a Congolese escort.[42] Léopoldville employed this control measure to discriminate against and harass the MPLA. In 1962 the MPLA was often impeded from reaching the border, and its arms confiscated, whereas the UPA/FNLA was accorded privileged and unimpeded access. Despite advantages in the international fora and on the battlefield, Roberto proved unable to lead effectively in either the political or the military dimension, and Léopoldville sponsorship was unable to reverse this trend.

From the beginning the MPLA had been unwelcome in Léopoldville, and so in June 1963 it moved its headquarters to Brazzaville. Its ability to project itself militarily into Angola became almost completely circumscribed by November, and it looked more and more isolated. In January 1964, at its Conference of Cadres (*Conferência de Quadros*) in Brazzaville, it was decided to begin rebuilding the movement as a serious revolutionary force. Part of this plan involved opening a front in the east of Angola through Zambia. The MPLA had made overtures to Kenneth Kaunda, the first president of Zambia following its independence from Britain in 1964. It had also befriended Nyerere, the first president of Tanzania, likewise following its independence from Britain in 1962. These relationships were to prove fortuitous. Beginning in 1965, Tanzania and Zambia permitted the transit of Chinese and Soviet weapons and MPLA cadres across their

territories to the Angolan border. This hospitality was likewise extended to Savimbi and UNITA. Because of this access, the MPLA and UNITA were able to open a major offensive and to conduct intensive insurgent campaigns in the eastern Angolan districts of Moxico and Cuando Cubango. Preparations were begun accordingly, and by the opening months of 1966 proselytizing of the population in the east was evident. The first armed incursions were detected in April: the war had now clearly shifted to the east of Angola and Portuguese resources were redirected to the east and southeast of the territory in response to the new threat.

Agostinho Neto chose his trusted associate, Daniel Chipenda, to lead the eastern offensive, and under his leadership events moved swiftly. The supply chain in support of this offensive began with Nyerere in Dar es Salam, through which arms flowed from communist bloc supplier-states. Dar es Salam was not only an arms port of entry but also the primary centre for training armed elements of the African National Congress (ANC), South West Africa People's Organization (SWAPO), Zimbabwe African People's Union (ZAPU), Zimbabwe African National Union (ZANU), MPLA and FRELIMO.[43] From this centre of mischief, armed and trained MPLA insurgents flowed to eastern Angola over a lengthy trail that wound through Tanzania and Zambia for nearly 600 miles, to Lusaka. From here there was a northern route of another 240 miles that served forces entering the Cazombo Salient and a southern one of about 180 miles that supplied thrusts both across the Cuando River and along the Zambezi River into Angola. The Salient is the large, approximately square geographical protrusion that is bounded by Zaire/Democratic Republic of the Congo (DRC) and Zambia on three sides and measures about 145 miles per side. It is crossed diagonally by the Zambezi, which ultimately flows through Zambia, over Victoria Falls and through Mozambique to the Indian Ocean. Because of its shape, exposed borders and remoteness, it was vulnerable to insurgent incursions.

In April 1966, following an intense effort to proselytize the population in the east, first in the district of Moxico and later in Cuando Cubango, the MPLA infiltrated a large group of combatants into the Cazombo Salient.[44] These troops showed a remarkable improvement over earlier Portuguese experience in subverting the population and employing selective terror when it did not cooperate. Subversion of the population in the east was estimated to be a modest six per cent in 1965 and about 42 per cent in 1968, the year that the MPLA offensive attained its height.[45]

In October 1966, after penetration of the Cazombo Salient, there was a surge of activity to the south next to the Zambian border and about 225 miles southeast of Luso. This area is more than 600 miles from the Atlantic Ocean, and the settlement of Luiana in the extreme southeast is equidistant from Luanda on the Atlantic and Beira on the Indian Ocean. This remoteness and the fact that the temperate savannah climate of central Angola, as it spreads south into this area with its lower altitude, becomes extremely harsh and desiccated, created a difficult operating environment. Conditions here favoured the insurgent in that he was easily able to detect Portuguese forces at considerable distance and did so generally before they were aware of him.

This insurgent advantage made it difficult for Portuguese forces to find and destroy the enemy. Like the frustrating bush of northern Angola, the terrain of the east had its own mysteries, and these would be unravelled through imaginative Portuguese solutions that relied on age-old skills mated with advanced training and modern technology.

1 René Pélissier, *La Colonie du Minotaure, Nationalismes et Révoltes en Angola (1926–1961)* [Colony of the Minotaur, Nationalism and Revolts in Angola] (Orgeval: Editions Pélissier, 1978), p. 658.

2 Hélio Felgas, *Guerra em Angola* [War in Angola] (Lisbon: Livraria Clássica Editora, 1961), p. 109.

3 John A. Marcum, *The Angolan Revolution: Volume I, The Anatomy of an Explosion (1950–1962)* (Cambridge: MIT Press, 1969), p. 228.

4 Ibid.

5 Ibid, p. 229.

6 Ibid, p. 230. The UPA/FNLA insurgents spoke mostly French, and this limitation made communicating with the local people difficult and proselytism even more so.

7 Ibid, p. 229.

8 Ibid.

9 Inge Brinkman, ;Refugees on Routes, Congo/Zaire and the War in Northern Angola (1961–1974)', paper delivered at the international symposium *Angola on the Move: Transport Routes, Communication, and History*, Berlin, 24–26 September 2003, p. 9.

10 Ibid.

11 Ibid.

12 Ibid.

13 Marcum, p. 229.

14 Ibid.

15 Ibid, p. 230.

16 Ibid, p. 231.

17 Brinkman, p. 3.

18 Marcum, p. 196.

19 Ibid.

20 Brinkman, p. 3.

21 Ministry of Foreign Affairs, *Portuguese Africa: An Introduction* (Lisbon: Ministry of Foreign Affairs, 1973), p. 73.

22 Colonel da Souza, interview by Al J. Venter in *The Terror Fighters: A Profile of Guerrilla Warfare in Southern Africa* (Cape Town: Purnell & Sons, 1969), p. 129.

23 Colonel (Engineers) Armando Girão, *10 Batalhões de Engenharia em Angola ... Antes da Subversão* [10 Engineering Battalions in Angola ... Before the Subversion] (Lisbon: Instituto de Altos Estudos Militares, 1965), Annex.

24 Brinkman, p. 6.

25 Ibid.

26 Ibid.

27 Ibid, p. 7.

28 Ibid.

29 Marcum.

30 Ibid, p. 230.

31 Ibid, p. 238. Batista was killed in a 6 February 1962 raid on a Portuguese camp near Bembe when UPA/FNLA forces were surprised in finding unanticipated and prepared Portuguese forces far outnumbering their attackers. Batista's death represented at a minimum a failure of UPA/FNLA intelligence.

32 Edgar Pereira da Costa Cardoso, *Presença da Força Aérea em Angola* [Presence of the Air Force in Angola] (Lisbon: Secretaria de Estado de Aeronáutica, 1963), p. 265.

33 Ibid., pp. 266-9.

34 Ibid, p. 269.

35 Ibid, p. 268.

36 George M. Houser and John A. Marcum, 'Joint Press Statement', Overseas Press Club, New York, 1 February 1962; and George M. Houser, 'A Report on a Journey through Rebel Angola', American Committee on Africa, New York, 1 February 1962. See also Marcum, *The Angolan Revolution*, pp. 228-32.

37 José Manuel Correia, 'Angola, Recordando 1961 e o Início da Actividade da Esquadra 93 "Magníficos"' [Angola, Rembering 1961 and the Beginning of Operations of Squadron 93 'The Magnificent Ones'], *Mais Alto* 395 (January–February 2012), p. 22.

38 Tomás George Conceição e Silva, 'The Portuguese Air Force in the African Wars of 1961–1974' in *Memories of Portugal's African Wars, 1961–1974*, ed. John P. Cann (Quantico: Marine Corps University Foundation, 1998), pp. 116-7.

39 Ibid.

40 Inge Brinkman, 'War and Identity in Angola', *Lusotopie 2003*, p.198.

41 Ibid.

42 John A. Marcum, *The Angolan Revolution, Volume II: Exile Politics and Insurgent Warfare (1962–1976)* (Cambridge: MIT Press, 1978), p. 42.

43 Dalila Cabrita Mateus, *A PIDE/DGS na Guerra Colonial 1961–1974* [The PIDE/DGS in the Colonial War 1961–1974] (Lisbon: Terramar, 2004), p. 283.

44 António Pires Nunes, *Angola 1966–1974, Vitória Militar no Leste* [Angola 1966–1974, Military Victory in the East] (Lisbon: Prefácio, 2002), p. 21.

45 Ibid, p. 6.

CHAPTER THREE:
THE BUSHMEN

When the insurgents found a sanctuary in Zambia and moved their operations to the east of Angola in 1966, they were then operating in an enormous area of some 420,000 square miles, more than seven and a half times the size of continental Portugal and six times the reclaimed area in the north, where they had been contained and largely expelled.[1] This was a wasteland for proselytizing, as there were only 1.3 million inhabitants in this eastern theatre or about three people per square mile. This figure was misleading, as the bulk of the population lived along the CFB or in the primary towns, so in the bush there was actually less than a person per square mile. The enemy goal, of course, was to penetrate far enough westward where there was a denser population that would respond to the insurgent message and a significant commercial infrastructure to attack. The problem with this approach was that it was a long and forbidding route to the developed area along the Atlantic seaboard and much could go wrong.

This eastern area is a vast plain with an altitude of about 3,000 feet. Within it there are two elevations, one in Bié and the other in the Cazombo Salient, where the land rises irregularly to about 5,000 feet.[2] It is a sprawling and difficult terrain that posed significant intelligence problems, for it meant that finding an insurgent column or small combat group in this setting was extremely complicated, and gathering the vital intelligence about its activities and intentions was an extraordinary challenge. The intelligence services needed new tools to accomplish their task and employed many imaginative methods designed to locate these small enemy elements that could easily elude the authorities and lose themselves in the bush. While the insurgents were relatively well adapted to the environment, the Portuguese were not and thus sought a way to bridge this gap. One of the most effective and among the most feared by the insurgents was the specialized Flecha troops, who were Bushmen hunter-gatherers native to the southeast of Angola, so named for their primary weapon, a poison-tipped arrow. They had thrived in the bush for thousands of years and knew the environment intimately. The story of how they converted their hunting skills into an armed, potent and feared intelligence-gathering competence is a remarkable journey.

Intelligence vision

Gaining intelligence on the insurgents was vital in keeping them separated from the population, denying them food, shelter and intelligence on military operations, and destroying them. The insurgents in all cases tended to frustrate the traditional intelligence processes, as there was only a loose link between decisions at the political level made at a headquarters in a sanctuary country and the activities of the military commanders in the field in Angola. This disconnect was due to the vast physical distances involved, the absence of any radio communications, and indiscipline in the field.[3] Thus, any intelligence generated on the strategic level needed to be verified and refined at the tactical level, making local intelligence critical.

Prior to the conflict, this local intelligence was generated through the army and the local and national police forces; however, the system had a number of weaknesses in its fragmentation and poor coordination. After March 1961, a Service of Centralization and Coordination of Intelligence (*Servico de Centralização de Informacoes*, or SCCI) was created in Angola to coordinate the activities of all intelligence-gathering organs. PIDE was a part of this organization and shared operational intelligence with it. PIDE operated quite differently in the *ultramar* from the *metrópole* in that it was very focused on gathering intelligence on nationalist organizations and their military wings as opposed to its political orientation in Lisbon. PIDE and its successor, in 1969, the *Direcção Geral de Segurança* (DGS), normally performed the various police and security duties that would typically fall to the British MI-6, Special Operations Executive, Scotland Yard's Special Branch Officers, or the US Federal Bureau of Investigation and Central Intelligence Agency. When the war began, the new requirements in Africa attracted the best talent in PIDE for this purpose. In Angola, it saw itself as a professional intelligence organization with links to the national intelligence agencies in Malawi, Rhodesia (Central Intelligence Organization, or CIO) and South Africa (Bureau of State Security, or BOSS). It also had a covert operations element that was engaged in espionage in the Congo, Zambia and Tanzania. PIDE/DGS faced initial problems in adjusting to the new environment and to gathering intelligence on insurgent movements in Angola. The population continued to be terrorized, the local situation remained confused and there was a consequent pressing need for a long-term solution. PIDE/DGS continued to experiment with this uncertain situation in its search for the key. One obstacle to its efforts was the diversity of languages, as there were perhaps 15 different dialects. By about 1967, in an attempt to make its reconnaissance missions more effective, it began to use local auxiliaries with their knowledge of the immediate terrain, familiarity with the population and unique language skills. This initiative proved partially successful.

As the MPLA, the UPA/FNLA and UNITA threatened the east, a young PIDE/DGS inspector, Óscar Cardoso, began examining innovative ways to gather intelligence on these organizations, particularly through the use of such units as the 'pseudo-gangs' of Kenya or the later Selous Scouts of Rhodesia.[4] He was deeply influenced by the writings of Jean Larteguy, Spencer Chapman, T.E. Lawrence, Mao Tse-Tung, and Sun Tzu on war, and specifically on insurgency and studied the nationalist movements assiduously.[5] Previously he had worked in counterintelligence and, through a series of assignments in the *ultramar*, had developed a deep understanding of Angola.[6] His interest in both insurgency and Angola combined to create a compelling professional fascination that drew him to the remoteness of Cuando Cubango for seven years and, in his words, "To say that I liked being there is insufficient – I adored being there."[7]

Earlier in 1965, in a café in Luanda, Cardoso had met Manuel Pontes, an administrator in Cuando Cubango who had a profound understanding of the eastern Angolan locale and its people. He spoke to Cardoso of the "lands at the end of the earth", a label that Henrique Galvão had given the area in his 1942 book, *Other Lands, Other People*.[8] Pontes had lived the majority of his life in the bush and described an ethnic minority in Cuando Cubango that the Portuguese called Bushmen (*Bosquímanos*). Cardoso knew of these people, for earlier he had held an academic chair in ethnography at the Graduate Institute of Colonial Studies (*Instituto Superior de Estudos Ultramarinos*). These Bushmen, or *Khum*, as they called themselves, survived as hunter-gatherers, and as their folklore described, *Kxau* was the first man created by their god, *Khu*, who also gave *Kxau* a wife, *Zan*. Evil threatened his man

Manuel Pontes on the Cuando River. *Photo Personal archive of Óscar Cardoso*

Óscar Cardoso (extreme left) with Manuel Pontes (extreme right), eastern Angola. *Photo Personal archive of Óscar Cardoso*

and woman, so *Khu* promised them that he would care for them and his loved ones by teaching them how to hunt, make poisoned arrows, dig with sharpened sticks for edible roots and use reeds to reach water below the surface.[9]

As Cardoso's interest in the concept of using them as intelligence gatherers heightened, he approached his senior, the director of PIDE in Angola, Dr Aníbal de São José Lopes. Lopes agreed that Cardoso should explore this possibility and authorized him to do so. Shortly thereafter, in the closing months of 1965, Pontes,

Cardoso, and his wife Irene drove into the bush of Cuando Cubango in a decrepit Land Rover to meet the Bushmen.[10]

The Bushmen

Earlier there had been efforts to recruit the local population and particularly Bushmen; however, this initiative had not been successful because they had a well-established fear of outsiders. Pontes's help represented a breakthrough, for he had lived modestly among these people for many years and held their confidence. He

A Bushman hunting. *Photo Personal archive of Óscar Cardoso*

made his home on a raft moored to the bank of the Cuando River, which defined part of the frontier with Zambia. The Bushmen not only respected him but felt a near adoration of him, so much so that they called him *Tata Khum*, which in their language meant 'Father of the *Khum*'.[11] When they saw him with his white beard, they lost their shyness and were delighted to speak. Afterward, Pontes told Cardoso, "If you train them, if they are fed well, these individuals will be very useful."[12] Cardoso agreed.

The Bushmen were and remain a very thin and small people with an average height of about four and a half feet and have a yellow-skinned oriental appearance. Their facial structure is particularly Asian and often features Mongolian eyefolds and a broad, flat face with almost no nose. While their skin is yellow, under the blazing sun, dust and sweat, it turns a copper brown with the exception of the underarm areas.[13] The only feature that they hold in common with the Negro or Bantu people is their peppercorn curly hair.[14] Elizabeth Marshall Thomas, an anthropologist who did ground-breaking work on the Bushmen, calls them handsome, because they move with remarkable grace, "strong and deft and lithe".[15] Bushmen are built for running and are consequently lean, muscled and fine-boned.[16] Their bare feet are hard and brown.

In 1966 there were about 47,000 Bushmen on the African subcontinent, an estimated 4,700 of whom were in the east of Angola.[17] The larger population spoke several dialects within the Khoisan language group, which is composed largely of the click languages spoken in southern Africa. This takes its name from the sharp clicks and pops made with the tongue in various parts of the mouth, combined with an implosion of breath.[18] For an outsider it is very difficult to understand and requires a native interpreter, as non-Bushmen have difficulty learning the language and are often misunderstood.[19] Conversely, the Bushmen were every bit as intelligent as Europeans and were able to learn Portuguese and speak it fluently, even with a perfect Lisbon accent.[20]

When Cardoso met the Bushmen, they had been settled in southern Africa for more than ten millennia. They retained their primitive habits, and made their necessities from things of the bush. Their tools were of wood or bone and their clothes were the skins of animals. The men wore only a leather loincloth, while the women wore a small leather apron and a large leather cape.[21] They were a neat and tidy people. Although their curly hair broke off naturally, they preferred it close-cropped. They had few possessions, as they lived a nomadic life with no permanent settlements.

Because water was scarce, they had no livestock or domestic animals, and most groups did not even have dogs. Instead of herding, they hunted. Their camps were comprised of no more than 20 to 25 people who represented a family nucleus. This usually consisted of an elder and his wife, their daughters and husbands and sometimes an unmarried son or two.[22] The small groups and constant moving had everything to do with finding food. Once the roots and berries were exhausted locally, a family relocated to harvest and hunt anew.

For the Bushman hunting was an art unto itself. They were hardy and tough and could endure prolonged hunger and thirst in chasing an antelope, their game of choice, stalking and shooting it and then tracking it for as long as several days before it died. The skills developed to do this required practised observation and heightened sensory perception. A Bushman could follow the spoor of his wounded antelope and recognize it among the spoor of its herd. He could track game over the hardest ground and know the individual footprints of his prey. He instinctively knew if bush or grass had been disturbed or a stone dislodged.[23] Even a child could recognize his mother's footprints, identify an edible root in the bush or see a scorpion hidden in the dust of a trail.[24] A Bushman could even detect a human scent and other invisible clues when tracking a human. He could tell you whether the tracks were made by a man or a woman, a black or a European, a person carrying a load or not.[25] He could find and follow a seemingly invisible track and do so at a rapid pace and at times at a run. Major Deville Linford, South African Defence Force (SADF), recalled a Bushman's revealing comment from his 1973 appointment as liaison officer to the Portuguese sector commander headquartered at Serpa Pinto in eastern Angola, "The whites can look but they can't see."[26] No other people had such tracking skills.

When a Bushman left his group to hunt, and evening came, he would sleep along a trail or in natural shelter of some kind, lying on his side with one ear to the ground and the other to the atmosphere in order to listen in both mediums. He could hear a man walking over a mile away and would be awakened.[27] Linford also remembers, "They could sleep like logs and often required shaking to wake them in the mornings," and yet he had once been woken by them in the early hours, before dawn, and told that the enemy was approaching.[28] It was often quite cold, and because the Bushman's animal skins did not protect him well, he would build a fire for warmth using friction. In the morning when he left, there would be a small pile of ash and perhaps a few footprints as the only signs of his presence.[29] Because the animal skins did not hold body heat, the Bushmen, when they became Flechas, traded the skins for cloth clothing that conformed to their bodies better and insulated them from the cold.

In hunting, the Bushmen used a small bow with a string made of antelope tendon and a short arrow with a bone-head. The arrowhead was coated with a terrible poison extracted from a certain grub and for which there was no known antidote. The poison affected the central nervous system, and paralysis of the prey developed quickly and progressively. With a well-placed arrow, the prey would die within a day. With a poor shot, death might take up to four days.[30]

About 3,000 years ago, the Bantu migration waves, originating in the Great Lakes region, pushed southward into the areas occupied by Bushmen. These invaders came with their superior weapons and great herds of cattle, and the Bushmen were forced to yield to the stronger newcomers. Many were killed, and the survivors were either enslaved or driven into the more remote areas where they could find safety. These areas were unsuitable for grazing,

Bantu with Bushman servant 1865, by Thomas Baines
William Fehr Collection, Castle of Good Hope, Cape Town

Bushmen practising with the Lee-Enfield rifle. Note the canvas shoes dyed with coffee. *Photo Personal archive of Óscar Cardoso*

as they had little water or fodder, and were thus unattractive to the Bantu. The Bushmen lived in fear of the hated Bantu, and as a result remained a shy people. Their grass huts were naturally camouflaged, easily constructed, and quickly abandoned under threat. After moving to safety, Bushmen could erect an entire encampment in short order. Because of their spartan lifestyle, the Bushman had few possessions to gather up and carry, a characteristic that made him very mobile and able to flee danger successfully. The Bantu abused the Bushmen, particularly those taken as slaves. As an example, in a society in which status is evidenced by clothes, the Bantu forced the Bushmen to remain almost naked with their traditional loincloth. This, in addition to other needless and demeaning treatment, caused extreme bitterness and hatred of the Bantu, and because the modern enemy was Bantu, Cardoso was able to use this long-standing animosity as a compelling motivation in recruiting Bushmen to hunt insurgents.[31]

Early operations

Cardoso's initial Bushman unit consisted of eight 'old' men, old because they were about 40 years old, which was the life expectancy of a Bushman.[32] Later there were always ample recruits, and Cardoso could pick from a broader selection. At first, PIDE/DGS used the Bushmen as trackers, for they could examine the ground and know everything. They were taken to Rivungo and other border areas where there were known insurgent infiltrations and from there tracked the insurgents to their encampments and arms caches. As they were armed only with their bows and poisoned arrows, they were not to engage the enemy, unless it was clear that they would prevail. The idea was

not to kill the intruders but simply to identify arms caches and collect documents from abandoned encampments. They were also to locate active encampments, identify the hut of the leader, count the number of men, and report on enemy activities.[33] All this was to be done covertly, and any military operations were to be left to formal Portuguese forces. Logistics on these missions were never an issue, as the Bushmen could find water and eat cockroaches.[34] They had learned from childhood to live on nothing. Willem Steenkamp, a former soldier and Cape historian, describes the Bushmen as "tireless, able to exist on the smell of an oil rag, could conceal themselves in the minimum of cover and seemed to have a built-in sense of direction, so that they never got lost, even in unfamiliar terrain."[35]

Cardoso's concept of the Flechas was to oppose the insurgents with a force of men who were comfortable with the wild and could live off the land.[36] This absence of logistic requirements made their presence and tactical movements easier and far less expensive than any conventional force. Later, when they were issued field rations so that they would spend their time hunting the enemy and not food, they would eat them all in a single sitting. Observers were invariably startled to see such small men consuming vast quantities of food and then not eating again for a week or more.

Bushmen were at times sent to very remote sites to locate insurgents and arms, though these missions had mixed results. Geographical references were poor, so it was difficult for the Bushmen to pinpoint the location of the enemy in their debrief, as the terrain tended to be very flat and featureless. Fortunately, the enemy encampments were either at the headwaters of a river or at the confluence of two rivers, for the insurgents would follow the river courses as an easy reference in finding their way into

Angola. The question for the debriefing officer then became one of geographic definition and orientation so that he could instruct Portuguese forces in planning an attack. PIDE found that it helped to give detailed instructions to the Bushmen so that they knew what was important in order to reduce vagueness and increase specificity. Also, it was difficult to march a prisoner long distances and have him survive under the sparse living conditions of the Bushmen. As PIDE/DGS and the Bushmen learned and adjusted, intelligence operations became smoother and more successful, although PIDE/DGS had seen impressive results from the start.

On the occasions in which Bushmen came in direct contact with one or two of the enemy, the traditional bow and arrow was effective. When hit by the poisoned arrowhead, the insurgent would collapse in a frozen but conscious and aware state. Driven by hatred, the Bushmen were known to slowly carve up the defenceless and vulnerable Bantu enemy until he died. In one debrief, a Bushman described how he had taken the beating heart from the chest of the victim and bitten it, while the immobile Bantu watched in excruciating pain as he died.[37] While this behaviour was forbidden, it did not stop the Bushmen from detesting the blacks with enormous passion and calling them *goubas*, or 'black cockroaches of the bush'. Interestingly, the Bushmen could smell the 'cockroaches' some distance off and were unlikely to be surprised by them.[38] They also had an uncanny ability to smell landmines.[39] In confirming the number of enemy killed, it became occasional practice for the Bushmen to return from these early missions with a bag of enemy ears as proof of success. The nature of these operations made the Bushmen much feared by the insurgents and this powerful message was reinforced as the mutilated corpses of their comrades were regularly discovered. This worked both ways, as when the insurgents located a Bushman encampment, they would massacre everyone, including elders, women and children.[40]

Originally, the Bushmen operated alone and not in direct coordination with or support of formal Portuguese forces. Their reconnaissance missions were wide-ranging, deep-penetration patrols in known or suspected enemy areas and were spartan and low profile. This independence would change as their unique skills became appreciated and helped to bridge a gap between conventional Portuguese forces and the local terrain, its people, and their culture. The army developed great respect for the Flechas, and as joint operations became a natural development, operated with them frequently, either in small reconnaissance groups or in larger contingents as part of an army operation. The Flechas were always best in tracking and fighting independently in small groups, as they had their own way of doing things; however, when fighting alongside traditional forces, and particularly the commandos, the two complemented each other well, and such coordinated operations were devastating to the enemy.

When Flechas operated with the army, they reported to the local army commander and were used to guide conventional troops. The army also relied on the Flechas to maintain the continuity of local operating knowledge in an area, as the overall experience

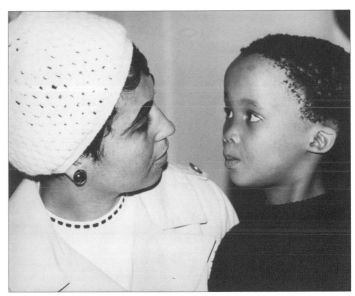

Irene Cardoso and an adopted Khum girl who survived a Bantu massacre. *Photo Personal archive of Óscar Cardoso*

level of a typical unit tended to degrade with the constant rotation of its troops.[41]

The Flechas were held in a sort of awe by the regular forces and this respect is best illustrated by the observations of a young subaltern, *Alfres* Filipe Silva, 4th Combat Group (platoon), 3rd Company, Infantry Battalion 4611. His unit, together with three other combat groups from his battalion, the 36th Company of Commandos and Flechas from the PIDE/DGS posts of Cuito Cuanavale, Mavinga and Mavengue, participated in Operation Zeus I. The operation ran from 3–12 March 1973 and was designed to eliminate the insurgent threat in a triangular area, bounded to the east by the road between Mavinga and Luengue, with boundaries running northwest from these two points to the confluence of the Cuzizi and Lomba rivers, a point approximately 43 miles west of Mavinga. Silva's combat group was augmented by a combat group of Flechas from Mavinga, and they assembled on the airfield there to begin the operation. All were issued field rations for the ten days; the Flechas promptly ate all of theirs, much to the shock of Silva and his men.

The next day when the mission began, Silva divided his troops into two groups, one of Flechas and the other of regular troops, as he had witnessed a great deal of unruliness, loud talking and clicking sounds among the Flechas, with no caution to the possibility of alerting the enemy. He was uncertain of them and their ways and was taking no chances. During the first night when all were encamped, each of the Flechas made a blazing fire and loudly chatted with each other, making nonsensical clicking noises. The rowdiness and firelight of the Flechas continued into the night and was certain to attract any enemy force. Certainly any hope of surprise was lost. Suddenly, all was silent and two or three Flechas turned their heads up and sniffed the air like dogs. There was more clicking, and then all rose and silently disappeared, on the run, into the bush and the dark. No more was seen of them for the remainder of the operation. They would send intelligence by radio of their progress in pursuing seven enemy insurgents whom they had identified and were pressuring relentlessly. At the end of the exercise, Silva saw two dead insurgents lying naked in the grass. Presumably the other five had escaped or had been killed, as he did not see them.[42] Alongside conventional forces, the Flecha style could be disconcerting.

The capability of the Flechas to operate covertly, even in relatively large combat groups of 25, could surprise other, regular forces and be quite unnerving. In another instance, Silva describes an operation, again in 1973, in which he was with a supply column moving between Cunjamba (Dima) and Mavinga. As was the custom, he was riding in a Mercedes-Benz Unimog leading the column as point and accompanied by four other men, who together comprised a hunting team. He was calmly following the road that ran along the edge of a *chana*, when the column was overflown by two T-6 Harvard armed trainer aircraft skimming low over the terrain and following the path of the road.[43] The two circled again and began to make diving manoeuvres around a zone to the front of the column. On their next pass they clearly indicated an area of interest by wagging their wings. When the Unimog was about 200 metres from the spot, Silva began to see uniformed individuals crossing the road and was paralyzed for a fraction of a second, thinking, "We have entered the jaws of the wolf!" His crew sprang to life and trained the vehicle-mounted machine gun onto the road, ready to fire. Silva's men stopped short when one of the individuals informed him that they were Flechas from Mavinga and that their radio had ceased to function. Apparently

they had neither food nor ammunition after an extended period in the field, and were thus quite vulnerable. *Comandante* Serpa, their leader, requested transport for his combat group to Mavinga to rearm and refit quickly. The previous day they had made contact with the enemy, and both had exhausted their ammunition on each other and withdrawn. Had the Flechas not been crossing the road and been seen by the aircraft, they would have remained invisible, and Silva and his men would never have known of their presence. As Silva noted, "It was quite a scene …"[44]

Bushmen to Flechas

The Bushmen gave the insurgents no rest night or day, constantly pursuing them, working their way close to the enemy, shooting and then disappearing. The insurgents would panic and loose off bursts from their Soviet Kalashnikov AK-47 battle rifles and attempt to pursue the Bushmen. When confronted in small groups, the insurgents were predisposed to surrender, as by and large they were not enthusiastic about dying for the nationalist cause. Larger groups of insurgents might flee, a decision that carried great risk in their becoming casualties.[45] If they stood and fought, and there was a serious gunfight in the engagement, the Flechas would extract themselves and melt into the bush, for they could easily be overwhelmed. On occasion, Flechas were captured and tortured. As these occurrences became more frequent, it became obvious that PIDE needed to train the Bushmen in modern warfare for their own protection and survivability and to arm them properly.

Flecha inspection. *Photo Personal archive of Óscar Cardoso*

Luanda: pearl of the South Atlantic, 1972. *Photo Personal archive of Mário Mendes*

A long-haul train negotiating a cut on the Benguela Railroad.

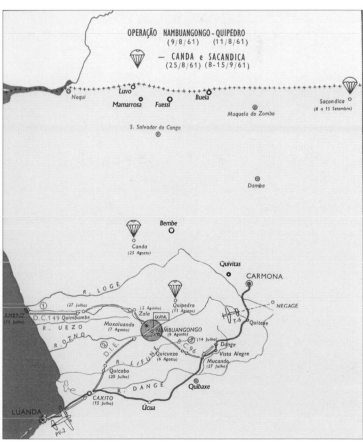

Northern Angola showing major operations.
Map Força Aérea Portuguesa

On the trail to the Lunguege River. *Photo Personal archive of Mário Mendes*

A typical trail through the bush of northern Angola.
Photo Personal archive of Mário Mendes

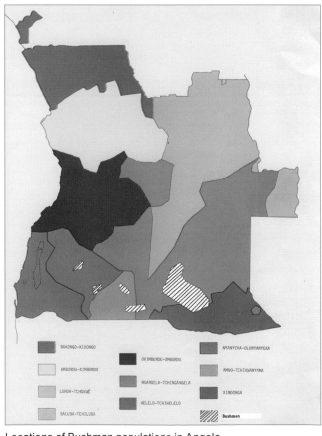

Locations of Bushman populations in Angola.
Photo Instituto de Investigação Cientifica de Angola

A flight of two T-6 armed trainers over Angola. *Photo Força Aérea Portuguesa*

A Flecha on patrol in eastern Angola, early 1970s.
Photo Personal archive of Óscar Cardoso

Óscar Cardoso instructing a Flecha in the use of a light machine gun.
Photo Personal archive of Óscar Cardoso

A Flecha posing with a Heckler & Koch G-3 battle rifle. *Photo Personal archive of Óscar Cardoso*

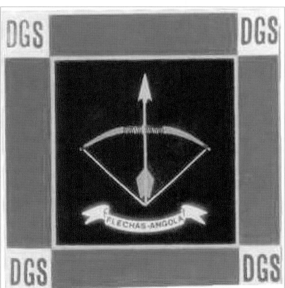

Flecha standard post-1969.
Photo Personal archive of Óscar Cardoso

A Flecha squad in eastern Angola.
Photo Jornal do Exército

This training began in Cuando Cubango at the prisoner work camp of Missombo, which was a rehabilitation centre for captured insurgents. The reservation was a sprawling, extensive 226,000 hectares, so there was ample room for both the Bushmen and insurgent prisoners.[46] It had a hospital and a school, and soon the Bushmen were learning to read and write. This training was the formal beginning of the Flechas.

Because it could be very cold and even at times below freezing in their operating areas, the Bushmen were initially given appropriate protective clothing, followed by the first uniforms which were makeshift, as adjustments and compromises were needed to accommodate them. Their small stature and mode of operations called for a tailored approach. There was much debate, for instance, on how uniforms would impair their tracking ability. As a compromise, they were issued very light-string canvas shoes with rope soles that were dyed brown with a coffee solution. This satisfied the social 'need' for a shoe but inhibited the Bushman's natural feel that his feet had developed with the ground. This contact was critical in their tracking role and, as such, they would abandon their new shoes to conduct patrols bare foot. Much later they were issued conventional uniforms and footwear, as once they had been exposed to the ways and habits of the formal Portuguese troops, there was a compelling desire to be like them. This occurred particularly in dress, as the Bushmen had long been denied this freedom. They wanted clothes, boots, sunglasses, a beret and all the other accoutrements of the modern soldier. Similarly to the shoes, sunglasses, while worn around the base and in off-duty time, were never worn on missions, as they were clumsy and interfered with their visual acuity.[47] Later the Bushmen were given their own distinctive camouflage-design beret when they graduated from training and became Flechas.

Military training to become a Flecha began with the development of shooting proficiency, as the Bushmen already had the necessary field skills. First, they tried the Lee-Enfield .303 bolt-action, magazine-fed, repeating rifle. It weighed 8.8 pounds and with its 44-inch length was too unwieldy for their small-framed bodies. When fired, its recoil was also heavy for them. It had been the standard of the British Army from 1895 to 1957, and an estimated 17 million were manufactured, so with its retirement, there was an ample supply. Still, it was unsuited and was replaced with the FAL (*Fusil Automatique Léger* or Light Automatic Rifle) 7.62mm, self-loading, selective-fire, battle rifle manufactured

Induction of a Bushman into the Flechas. The instructor (right) is about to place a captured enemy weapon in the hands of the new Flecha. Note the camouflage berets. *Photo Personal archive of Óscar Cardoso*

A Flecha ready for patrol in his coffee-dyed shoes. *Photo Personal archive of Óscar Cardoso*

33

by FN (*Fabrique Nationale de Herstal*). The FAL weighed 8.5 pounds and was 43 inches in length. Although weight and length of the Lee-Enfield and FAL were not too different, the FAL seemed to work better. There were, however, teething problems, as when automatic fire was selected, the Bushmen could not hold the FAL on target. When it was switched to semi-automatic, they achieved good results and became expert shots.[48] Indeed, they seemed to have an instinctive understanding of spatial relationships and ballistics. Flecha operations garnered a wealth of captured Soviet weaponry, and the Flechas found the AK-47 less cumbersome and easier to handle over other available weaponry. It proved simple, durable and reliable, and eventually replaced the FAL as the weapon of choice. It was relatively short at 34.3 inches, which compensated for its heavier 10.5-pound weight. The Flechas also used the standard Heckler & Koch G3 Portuguese battle rifle, which was manufactured under licence in Lisbon by the *Fábrica de Braço de Prata* as the *Espingarda m/961*. It was about the size and weight of the FAL at 9 pounds and 40.4 inches and was used primarily by non-Bushman Flechas. By 1974, standardization had begun on the lightweight US M-16, 5.56mm assault rifle, which was slightly longer at 39.5 inches but lighter at 7.2 pounds.[49]

Flechas being presented at a reception, well behaved but uncomfortable. *Photo Personal archive of Óscar Cardoso*

Flechas at their conversion. *Photo Personal archive of Óscar Cardoso*

Also in their training they learned to read maps and marked them in square sectors designated as A, B, C, D, etc. When they became more familiar with technology, they also learned to use the radio. As their training progressed, they would exercise Bushman on Bushman to hone their skills. In such exercises praise for a job well done from the Portuguese was not enough: praise had to come from fellow Bushmen to be meaningful.[50]

Training at Missombo was also inspired by the teachings of Sun Tzu, as quoted by Cardoso, "When campaigning, be swift as the wind, as impenetrable as the forest, as obscure and mysterious as the night; and attack with the suddenness of the flash and violence of thunder."[51] Accordingly, it was divided into two phases, day and night operations, each a complement to the other. Daylight operations emphasized stealth, and specialized night fighting proved a great success with its element of surprise.

During this initial training there arose a number of problems because of cultural adjustments. First, recruiting a Bushman and accepting him into the Flecha force meant his bringing his family, who needed to be housed and fed. This was very important to him and affected his performance in the field. Imaginative solutions were devised to convert these dependents into additional manpower, and utilize their skills.

For instance, the boys 12 years and older were employed as base guards.[52] Flechas received a small allowance to help in caring for their dependents, and they lived apart in their own enclaves with their families, where they dutifully erected a flagpole and flew the Portuguese flag. They were very disciplined, morally proper and were proud of their new life, the freedom to live, their status as human beings and their fatherland.[53] Portugal had dignified the Bushmen and protected their families, and for this it would receive their unqualified loyalty.

In the beginning, PIDE paid the Flechas in booty. Later when blacks were employed in the Flecha units, adjustments had to be made to quell the inherent ill feeling. For one, remuneration was changed in keeping with that of troops from the *metrópole,* and it was paid in cash. This had to be handled carefully, as many Flechas would immediately spend their earnings on drink and have little left to support their several wives and numerous children. As a consequence, multiple disbursements were made to families to avoid this pitfall.[54]

There were also a number of reasons for volunteering that were incompatible with the Flecha mission and image. In their new official status, many would sneak away from the camp and raid neighbouring villages to steal firearms and chickens. When Cardoso discovered this, he was forced to discipline those involved and explain that the war was not against blacks for the benefit of the Bushmen. Portugal's war was against those who wanted to make war, the insurgents and their organizations.[55]

Another incident centred on an incredible case of gluttony, perhaps as a result of the Bushman's traditional difficulty in finding food. When much of the population of eastern Angola fled to towns and cities for safety from the insurgents, they left their livestock in pasture. The cattle were vulnerable to lions and other beasts of prey, and to insurgent foraging. Cardoso sought to deny the enemy's living off the stray beef, so he ordered the Bushmen to locate the abandoned herds and move them to protected areas. This they did, but in doing so, each of these thin, delicate men, well under five feet tall, slaughtered a steer and consumed the entire carcass single-handedly. Indeed, they ate like animals, and Cardoso was forced to introduce a certain discipline into their habits.[56]

There was never a desertion in the Flechas. When they were tired of fighting or thought that they were too old, they would tell Cardoso, "*Senhor* Inspector, I am tired, I am old. I do not wish to fight any longer. Here is my weapon, I do not wish more."[57] They would become farmers on the small farm at Missombo, where the captured insurgents also worked, and live there with their families.

When training was completed, there was a formal induction into the Flechas. It was a ceremony full of significance, in which each candidate was presented with a weapon taken from the enemy which he accepted with his outstretched arms overlaid with the Portuguese flag. These were symbols of his dedication and loyalty to his country and the war that it was fighting.[58]

Another aspect of the Flechas newly acquired culture was their conversion to Christianity, specifically the Roman Catholic faith.

Flechas at a conversion service with G3 rifles, camouflage berets and the Flecha standard of Cuando Cubango.
Photo Personal archive Óscar Cardoso

Just as with the new aspects of their clothing, weaponry and social and political development, so they embraced religion with enthusiasm.

There were always more volunteers than there were opportunities in the force, and this situation continued throughout the war. Because the Flechas were so specialized, and managing the force of Bushmen with their unique family and personal requirements took much care and attention, the force would always be relatively small. By 1968 it had reached a level of about 600 Bushmen operating in Cuando Cubango. The formula had proved its effectiveness and supported its replication in other areas. In order to expand, PIDE/DGS began recruiting captured and turned MPLA insurgents and other local volunteers, primarily from the militias. These were used principally in the areas around Gago Coutinho, Luso and Carmona. There was no fixed routine in turning insurgent prisoners, as each was treated according to the circumstances. It all depended on his initial behaviour, cooperation and general demeanour. Cardoso sought people native to the affected areas, because they knew the terrain where they would operate, spoke the language and belonged to the local ethnic groups.[59]

Despite the relatively small numbers, the Flechas worked well with the Portuguese, and more were always needed. While the Flechas had their unique African way of solving problems, "they attained an elevated operational effectiveness", according to Brigadier Pedro Pezarat Correia, a veteran of Mozambique (two tours) and Guiné.[60] Similarly, Lieutenant-Colonel Ron Reid-Daly of the Rhodesian Selous Scouts Regiment called the Flechas "the best indigenous African shottists I came across during my army service in Africa".[61] The Flecha formula was also attempted in Mozambique and Guiné, but never with quite the same success as in Angola.

At the end of hostilities in 1974, there were only around 1,700 Flechas in the east of Angola and another 456 in the north, a total of 2,156.[62]

1   António Pires Nunes, *Angola, 1961–74: Vitória Militar no Leste* [Angola, 1961–74: Military Victory in the East] (Lisbon: Prefácio, 2002), pp. 6-10.

2   Ibid.

3   Renato F. Marques Pinto, 'Intelligence, The Key to Counterinsurgency' in *Memories of Portugal's African Wars, 1961–1974*, ed. John P. Cann (Quantico: Marine Corps University Foundation, 1998), p. 20.

4   Aniceto Afonso & Carlos de Matos Gomes, *Guerra Colonial* [Colonial War] (Lisbon: Editorian Notícias, 2000), p. 341.

5   See Jean Larteguy, *Les Centurions* (Paris: Presses de la Cité, 1960); F. Spencer Chapman, *The Jungle is Neutral: A Soldier's Two-Year Escape from the Japanese Army* (Singapore: Marshall Cavendish, 2003); T.E. Lawrence, *The Seven Pillars of Wisdom* (New York: Doubleday, 1935); Mao Tse-Tung, *On Guerrilla Warfare*, trans. Samuel B. Griffith (New York: Frederick Praeger, 1961); and Sun Tzu, *The Art of War*, trans. Samuel B. Griffith (London: Oxford University Press, 1963).

6   Óscar Cardoso, 'Criador dos Flechas' [Creator of the Flechas] in José Freire Antunes, *A Guerra de* África*, 1961–1974, Volume 1* [The War in Africa, 1961–1974, Volume 1] (Lisbon: Temas e Debates, 1996), p. 403.

7   Ibid.

8   Henrique Galvão, *Outras Terras, Outras Gentes: Viagens na África, 25,000 Kilometers em Angola* [Other Lands, Other Peoples: Travels in Africa, 25,000 Kilometers in Angola] (Porto: Emprêsa do Jornal de Notícias, 1942).

9   Cobus Venter, 'Bushman Battalion', http://www.samagte.co.za/weermag/31/31.html (accessed 28 June 2012), pp. 1-2.

10 Óscar Cardoso, interview by the author, 18 June 2012, Casal do Mogos, Santo Isidoro, Portugal.

11 Cardoso, p. 404.

12 Ibid.

13 Elizabeth Marshall Thomas, *The Harmless People* (New York: Vantage Books, 1989), p. 6.

14 Cardoso interview.

15 Thomas, p. 7.

16 Ibid.

17 Venter, pp. 1-2.

18 Thomas, p. 8.

19 Ibid., 9.

20 Cardoso interview.

21 Thomas, p. 7.

22 Ibid.

23 Ian Uys, *Bushman Soldiers, Their Alpha and Omega* (Germiston, South Africa: Fortress Publishers, 1993), p. 54.

24 Thomas, p. 13.

25 Cardoso interview.

26 Uys, p. 55.

27 Cardoso interview.

28 Uys, p. 55.

29 Thomas, p. 8.

30 Ibid., p. 9; Cardoso interview.

31 Cardoso interview.

32 Ibid.

33 Cardoso, p. 405.

34 Cardoso interview.

35 Willem Steenkamp, *South Africa's Border War, 1966–1989* (Gibraltar: Ashanti Publishing, 1989). p. 205.

36 Óscar Cardoso, correspondence with the author, 15 March 2013.

37 Cardoso, p. 405.

38 Cardoso interview.

39 Steenkamp, p. 205.

40 Cardoso interview.

41 Óscar Cardoso, interview by the author, 1 April 1995, Azaruja, Portugal.

42 Filipe Silva and Fernando Moreira, *Os Flechas* [The *Flechas*], Forum 4611, http://forum4611.blogspot.com/2012_10_01_archive.html (accessed 12 April 2013).

43 A *chana*, *xana*, or *anhara* is an Angolan (Umbundo) term that refers to flat, plain-like country with very low vegetation, normally grass. When *chanas* are crossed by rivers, they are frequently inundated, particularly in the rainy season.

44 Silva & Moreira.

45 Cardoso, p. 408

46 Ibid, p. 406.

47 Cardoso interview, 18 June 2012.

48 Ibid.

49 Cardoso interview, 1 April 1995.

50 Ibid.

51 Cardoso, p. 406; Sun Tsu, *The Art of War*, trans. Samuel B. Griffith (London: Oxford University Press, 1963), p. 106: Actual words are, "When campaigning, be swift as the wind; in leisurely march, majestic as the forest; in raiding and plundering, like fire; in standing, firm as the mountains. As unfathomable as the clouds, move like a thunderbolt."

52 Ibid.

53 Óscar Cardoso, 'Tribute to the veterans of the 31st Battalion and their commander Colonel Deville Linford', delivered on 24 September 2011, Pretoria, South Africa.

54 Cardoso interview, 18 June 2012.

55 Cardoso, p. 406.

56 Ibid.

57 Ibid.

58 José Victor de Brito Nogueira e Carvalho, *Era Tempo de Morrer em* África: *Angola, Guerra e Descolonização, 1961–1975* [It Was a Time to Die in Africa: Angola, War and Decolonization, 1961–1975] (Lisbon: Prefácio, 2004), p. 183.

59 Óscar Cardoso, correspondence with the author, 15 March 2013.

60 Pedro Pezarat Correia, '*A Participação Local no Desenvolvimento das Campanhas: O Reucrutamento Africano*' [Local Participation in the Expansion of the Campaigns] in *Estudos sobre as Campanhas de* África *(1961–1974)* [Studies on the African Campaigns], Instituto de Altos Estudos Militares, ed. (São Pedro Estoril: Edições Atena, 2000), p. 148.

61 R.F. Reid-Daly, *Pamwe Chete: The Legend of the Selous Scouts* (Johannesburg: Covos Day, 2001), p. 61.

62 Estado-Maior de Exército, *Resenha Histórico-Militar das Campanhas de* África *1961–1974, 6 Volume, Aspectos da Actividade Operacional, Tomo I, Angola–Livro 2* [Historical Military Report on the African Campaigns 1961–1974, 6 Volume, Aspects of Operational Activity, Tome I, Angola, Book 2] (Lisbon: Estado-Maior de Exército, 2006), p. 469.

CHAPTER FOUR:
FLECHA OPERATIONS

War in the east of Angola began in earnest in November 1966, when some MPLA insurgents penetrated the northeast corner of the Cazombo Salient near the border settlements of Jimbe and Caianda. UNITA also entered the fray, and Savimbi's first attack occurred in December 1966 on the post of Cassamba. He attacked again two weeks later on Christmas Eve, when 500 UNITA insurgents attacked the Portuguese garrison of Teixeira de Sousa and suffered a disastrous defeat with 234 dead. UNITA and the MPLA were soon alienated from their vital patron, as Portugal struck at the fragile Zambian treasury by closing the CFB to copper exports for a week. Again, in April 1967, there were two UNITA acts of sabotage on the CFB infrastructure, and again Portugal closed the railway and threatened lengthier closures unless attacks ceased. Thereafter UNITA was unwelcome in Zambia, and the MPLA was likewise put on notice not to interfere with the CFB.

Portuguese leverage had its roots in Zambian dependence on the CFB to export its copper ore across Angola. The railway always represented a tempting target for insurgents, and thus Zambia found itself caught between the practical need for foreign sales and the ideological desire to support nationalist movements. Several temporary closures, in December 1966 and again in the second quarter of 1967, as a result of attacks or acts of sabotage on the CFB, carried a strong message to both Zambia and the Congo. As a consequence, during early 1967, the MPLA was ostensibly pushed out of Zambia and infiltrated the east in two primary areas, Lake Dilolo on the western edge of the Salient, and a larger area located about 160 miles due south of Luso and bounded by the settlements of Sessa, Muié,

Cangombe and Cangamba. By 1968, this surge had penetrated as far west as the Bié district and, as a result of such over-extension, various MPLA columns found themselves quite vulnerable. Considerable numbers were destroyed or captured, but by 1970 there were still 1,300 men in Zambian bases and an estimated 3,850 running loose in Angola, creating trouble.[1] There were

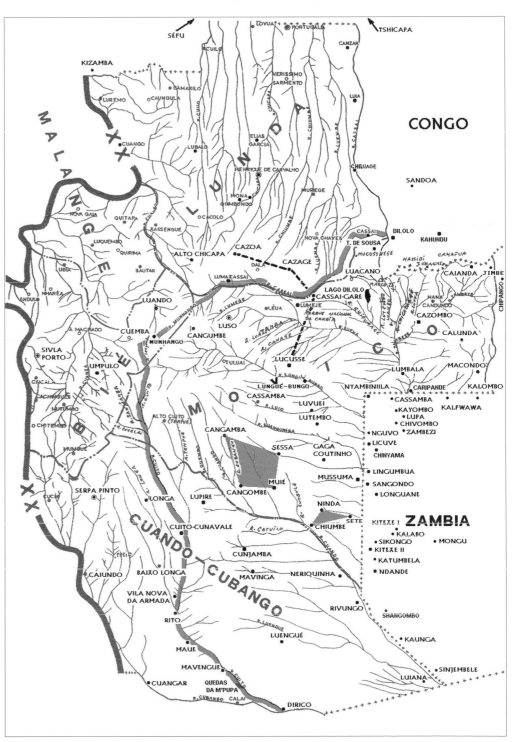

Eastern Military Zone, 1968, showing insurgent bases in Congo and Zambia.
Modified from a map by António Pires Nunes

clearly limits to diplomatic and economic pressure in the face of Kaunda's strong feelings toward African nationalist movements.

Correlation of forces

The MPLA was not alone in exploiting the east. The UPA/FNLA and its military wing, the ELNA, likewise saw the east as an alternative opportunity to the stalemate in the north and felt that it was losing politico-military ground to its competitors through inaction. The organization had fielded three battalions by 1970, following a regrouping from the *jacquerie* of 1961. These were launched separately into Angola from the north, the northeast and east in a general invasion. The northern group was, fortuitously for the Portuguese, discovered in concentration, and was destroyed by some vigorous Portuguese air force attacks.[2] The northeastern group crossed in force near Santa Cruz, a settlement some 360 miles northeast of Luanda, and was destroyed by several companies of commandos in one of the more brilliant operations conducted in Angola, *Operação Golpe de Flanco* or Operation Flank Attack.[3] The eastern group crossed from its base at Kahundu through Teixeira de Sousa, a primary border town and station for the CFB, to reinforce one of its groups already near Luacano and soon clashed with MPLA forces. The MPLA had a strong presence in the area and, after its earlier treatment by Léopoldville, was determined not to be displaced. The UPA/FNLA was humiliated in this engagement and consequently lost enormous face and prestige, as well as key international support from the OAU.[4] As 1970 drew to a close, the UPA/FNLA had approximately 6,000 men isolated in the north of Angola, in the nearly impenetrable Dembos forest region, of whom only about 2,000 were armed. The northeastern and eastern groups had ceased to exist as effective fighting forces.[5]

Savimbi was forced through circumstances into an improbable posture, claiming that a true nationalist movement should operate from bases within Angola. Perhaps this was a necessary policy, as in July 1967 he was finally and completely expelled from Zambia. Certainly the implementation of such a policy ensured his isolation. By 1969, UNITA was surrounded, and Savimbi counted fewer than 1,500 followers. In order to survive in defeat, he and his men came to an accommodation with the Portuguese. Between 1971 and 1973 UNITA activities were restricted to a prescribed zone at the headwaters

of the Lungué-Bungo River, and it had agreed to cease operations against the Portuguese.[6] As part of this understanding, UNITA would receive arms and medical support and would be free to engage MPLA forces.[7] By this time, Savimbi had a force of about 500, of which 250 were armed.[8]

In contrast, by December 1971, the army in the Eastern Military Zone had 55 infantry companies, two companies of commandos, two squadrons of cavalry, an artillery battery of 88mm field guns, two engineering companies and a construction company. There were also the Auxiliary Forces, consisting of three groups of *Fiéis*, or 'Faithfuls' (2,318 men), 71 groups of *Grupos Especiais,* or Special Groups (2,279 men), one group of *Leais*, or 'Loyals' (128 men), 31 groups of Flechas (1,665 men) and various armed militias (5,331 men), a total of 11,721 additional men over and above the approximately 7,500 regular forces.[9] Further, there were approximately 1,200 air force personnel and perhaps 300 naval personnel, bringing the total number of Portuguese forces in the east to about 20,700.[10] This number yields a ratio of 3.2 to 1 over the insurgent aggregate of 6,350 men. While comparable ratios of other counterinsurgencies were higher, such as, Malaya at 37.5 to 1, Cyprus at 25 to 1, Algeria at 16.7 to 1, Kenya at 4.6 to 1, Vietnam in 1964 at 4.1 to 1 and Vietnam in 1968 at 8.75 to 1, isolation of the insurgents in a sparsely inhabited and barren region belied the apparent weakness of this figure.[11]

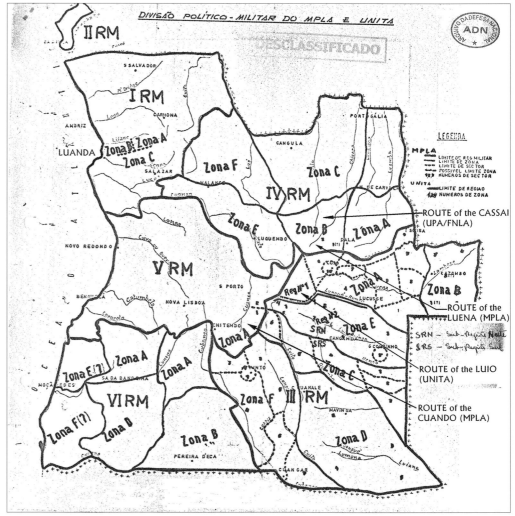

Insurgent military zones and incursion routes from eastern Angola. *Photo Arquivo da Defesa Nacional*

Insurgent strategy

The strategy of the nationalist movements was to seek independence for Angola through armed conflict rather than negotiation, although the UNITA strategy was less clear. Accordingly, the MPLA, from its Zambian bases, planned a two-pronged assault. The southern one would be mounted from Mongu, Shangombo and Sikongo and known as the Route of the Cuando, as shown on the map facing that depicts the UPA/FNLA, MPLA, and UNITA external bases and internal military zones. It would follow this river valley westward with the aim of reaching the populated and wealthy district of Bié and the central plain of Huambo, the heart of Angola. From this point the insurgents hoped to control the entire country and reach all the way to Malange through an axis of advance along the Cuanza River valley.[12]

The northern one was called the Route of the Luena, or the 'Agostinho Neto Route', by the MPLA. It was to be launched from Chipango and Cassamba and aimed directly at Luso and from there to the highland plain of Malange. The hope was to gain control of the Luanda–Malange railway, reach Luanda and link with forces coming from the north.[13] These routes, pushing out of the salient and following the Luena River, never successfully penetrated a front defined by an interior line connecting the population centres of Cazoa, Cazage, Cassai-Gare and Lucusse, with Luso as its hub.[14] The MPLA could muster about 4,000 men, of whom about 3,000 were armed. Its operations were centred around anti-vehicle and anti-personnel mines, forced recruiting and intimidation of the population, reaction to Portuguese operations and desultory bursts of fire at Portuguese military installations in hit-and-run tactics.[15] Flechas were to prove particularly useful in finding, tracking and helping eliminate MPLA insurgents originating in the salient.

Campaign plans for the UPA/FNLA are much less distinct. Its plan can be imputed from the attempt in 1970 to infiltrate three battalions in the north, with the goal of controlling the rich, coffee-growing region north of the Luanda–Malange railway and paralyzing the Angolan economy, an objective that had failed in 1961. This offensive action would presumably bring its forces to the gates of Luanda and precipitate a sudden conclusion to the conflict. The offensive was abandoned in September 1972 because UPA/FNLA forces were stalemated at the edge of Portuguese territory, checked by both the MPLA and the Portuguese in the north and east of the Eastern Military Zone, and thus stood little chance of success. Its forces in the northeast were estimated at 1,300 men, of whom 500 were armed, and in the east, 6,000 men, of whom 400 were armed.[16] Both groups remained relatively inactive as a means of survival.

UNITA simply intended to establish a base deep in the interior of Angola and, using some notion of the oil-spot theory of expanding control, mobilize an ever-increasing number of the population to gain the 'total independence of Angola'.

There were substantial weaknesses in the campaign design of all three, in that their lines of communication would be long and vulnerable or, in the case of UNITA, non-existent. The goals of each would rely increasingly on the feeble strategy of hope, as each moved farther and farther from its external support and progressively isolated itself deep in the hostile interior of Angola. If these organizations were going to rely on classic proselytizing of the population for support, then it would not come willingly. The Angolan people were experiencing new political and economic freedoms and financial prosperity and would hardly welcome what would be tantamount to Napoleonic-style foraging by foreign armies. Then too, the basic premise of all three insurgencies had been removed with successful responses to the people's grievances. Nationalism for the sake of nationalism and the political goal of a single-party state running a country for the benefit of its oligarchy or chief of state held little popular appeal. Lastly, the insurgents' greatest enemies were each other, as all three were in competition for the spoils to be mined from governing Angola. There was no thought of a coalition government for the greater good of the diverse population.

Portuguese counterinsurgency

In countering this multi-axis assault, the Portuguese were quick to see that UNITA and the UPA/FNLA would be easily contained and that the MPLA represented the real threat. They thus developed a three-phase, long-range theatre strategy of first checking the expansion of the insurgent penetration. This would mean defining the population battlefield and bringing security to those threatened. Next, the security forces would surround the insurgents and limit them to area bounded by the Cuito, Cuanza, Munhango and Cassai rivers, essentially a line running from Dirico in the south to Teixeira de Sousa in the northeast. This was admittedly a substantial tract, but it was thinly populated by any standard and would provide little sustenance. The insurgents could thus do little damage in such isolation and would indeed slowly starve. Within it Portuguese security forces would relentlessly pursue the enemy, who would become increasingly harried and besieged. Finally, in 1973 and 1974, as the cordon drew increasingly tight, the enemy would be completely destroyed.[17]

The need for this lengthy approach was prompted by a number of factors. First, Portugal had limited manpower to police the vast region of the east. This limitation dictated an approach that enlisted the sparse terrain, geographic remoteness and harsh climate as allies in isolating the insurgents in an attritional war. Second, these three regional characteristics appeared to favour the insurgent in that he could easily hide or move largely unhindered by Portuguese forces.

This freedom-of-movement problem was nowhere more evident than in the Chana da Cameia, a vast plain of some millions of square miles completely covered in tall grass. Its extension, vastness and lack of topographical references made it difficult to navigate and search for the enemy successfully. It was bounded in the north by the CFB and in the south by the Luena River, the Route of Agostinho Neto. In the rainy season it was largely impassable because of flooding, but in the dry season it could be easily crossed on foot, in vehicles or on horseback. Very few people lived in the Cameia, but the small numbers who did were forced to aid the MPLA. MPLA troops in transit through this *chana* alongside the Luena were difficult to find hiding in the grass and required tailored tactics to weed them out.

Another difficulty navigating eastern Angola lay in the hundreds of water courses that permeate the Angolan landscape. The vast riverine network made certain that any movement by either Portuguese forces or the enemy would involve one or more river crossings, some easily fordable and others extremely difficult. Portuguese forces learned to excel in negotiating this extensive river system. They developed the skills to cross any river, day or night, and to use it as a natural obstacle to enemy manoeuvre and as ideal defensive terrain. Rivers also served as natural boundaries to the battlefield and provided navigation references and orientation. They likewise proved to be avenues of enemy approach for combat and lines of communication for enemy incursions. These latter characteristics were to help in predicting the location and route of enemy incursions.

Because of the nature of the battlefield and the enemy, a containment strategy was well suited. It was one in which Portuguese forces defined and then gradually reduced the area of insurgent contamination, forcing the enemy to fight from a progressively reduced and isolated position and ultimately to face elimination. The few local people living in the east and southeast could hardly subsist themselves, much less support the insurgents with food, recruits, intelligence and shelter. In summary, Portuguese theatre strategy was based on sound reasoning, following a considered appraisal of opponent strengths, battlefield terrain and resident population. One of the keys to this strategy was the Flechas, who would gather intelligence in this difficult environment and lead larger, more formal and heavier Portuguese forces to the enemy.[18] They would

Helicopters refuelling during operations in the Cameia. *Photo António Pires Nunes, Siroco*

Hunting for the enemy by Jeep in the Cameia. *Photo António Pires Nunes, Siroco*

Hunting on foot in the immensity of the Cameia. *Photo António Pires Nunes, Siroco*

pursue him relentlessly and give him no rest. Within this framework, the PIDE/DGS expanded its network of informers and agents in the Congo and Zambia and established additional posts in the areas of penetration at Mussuma and Rivungo.[19]

Fearless bloodhounds

Flecha missions were handled by the PIDE/DGS and generally run from its local detachment offices or posts. Detachments from a centralized brigade headquarters were also deployed to various sites, and operations were staged from these, based on intelligence indicating a high probability of enemy presence, or confirming the same. The missions ranged in purpose from simply gathering intelligence on reconnaissance patrols, to capturing a prisoner

Flecha in the bush of eastern Angola. *Photo Estado-Maior do Exército*

Flechas on parade in eastern Angola.
Photo Personal archive of José Nogueira e Carvalho

for further interrogation or turning, to pathfinding for a heavier, regular force. The Flechas were quite flexible, and their role could be tailored accordingly. A mission to gather intelligence sought to locate abandoned enemy encampments, search them for documents and other clues as to insurgent intentions, count the number in the group, and determine its direction of travel. A mission to capture one or more insurgents had to be tailored to the size of the enemy group so that the Flechas would not be overwhelmed. A mission to destroy insurgents was used only in the case of a small, isolated group that could muster little firepower. Flechas were also used to protect a conventional force by scouting ahead and on its flanks for ambushes or to lead it to the exact location of the enemy.

Strategically, a primary role of the Flechas was to disrupt enemy logistic lines of communication, as insurgent logistics were a key limiting factor or critical vulnerability in the columns penetrating eastern Angola. These supply lines stretched over long distances from bases in the Congo and Zambia to the forces in the field and were consequently very fragile. Maintaining them was a complicated venture and, indeed, the MPLA had a department of logistics with its central headquarters in Lusaka. From here all matériel received was distributed according to the needs of the different MPLA military zones and regions in Angola.[20]

From stockpiles in the border areas, matériel flowed across the frontier, carried by insurgents or impressed porters and stored in caches as an inventory buffer to supply troops operating deep in Angola. The job of the Flechas was to locate these caches, and either destroy the weapons or otherwise remove them and thereby disrupt the supply chain and reduce the insurgents' ability to execute a campaign plan. Expending ammunition with no replacement source left insurgents extremely vulnerable, with few viable options other than to return to the safety of Zambia or to surrender to the Portuguese. By 1971, these logistic lines of communication, feeding into the Cazombo Salient, were being abandoned as unworkable and unsustainable, according to documents captured by the Flechas.[21] Portuguese forces were disrupting them with regularity, so much so that at first they were shortened and then, as the Flechas and regular forces took their toll, shifted to the south, where Portuguese presence was weaker. The MPLA campaign was thus adjusted to avoid Portuguese strength, and its primary logistics base was shifted from Cassamba, south to Kitexe II. This change aggravated the support problem and forced an adverse strategic adjustment on the MPLA. It was now necessary to move from the easier and more direct route to the Angolan heartland through the district of Moxico, to the sparsely populated and more distant one through Cuando Cubango.[22] These long distances through bleak and baking Bushman habitat, where there were relatively few natives to impress as porters, made for a difficult journey.

A Flecha operation against these supply lines generally began with the generation of intelligence on the enemy. While the army did not have an intelligence service of professionals, it had a system of intelligence, with divisions or sections at all headquarters commands, from the major staff level to the lower levels in the chain. These cells were manned by officers with a sub-specialty and schooling in intelligence, and thus there was a system functioning at all levels of command. It was supported by the air force, with visual and photographic reconnaissance and by radio-intercept detachments. PIDE/DGS was responsible for intelligence collecting abroad through its agents and informers and for counterintelligence internally or, in this case, countersubversion. The intelligence sections in the field handled prisoner debriefing to harvest immediately perishable information. The SCCI in Angola and Mozambique analyzed and evaluated the information from these various sources and produced intelligence that would drive operations against the insurgents.[23] From this formal source of intelligence the Flechas were briefed, prepared for the missions, and departed carefully and stealthily to pursue their business. Other sources might be more informal, such as an informer suddenly appearing or an insurgent surrendering. Information derived from these sources generally required prompt action because of its perishability. On a more practical note, the tactical interrogation of a prisoner conducted in the field by his captors, often in the heat of combat, sought to discover the whereabouts of his fellow insurgents, their intentions and their arms caches. The divulging of such important tactical intelligence frequently meant that prisoners were responsible for the killing or capture of their comrades, something that thoroughly compromised them.[24]

A mission surprise

José Nogueira e Carvalho, an agent in the PIDE/DGS at the time, describes from his personal experience a typical operation that originated in the village of Cuemba in the district of Bié, a small locale lost in the centre of Angola. His detailed account provides a flavour of the typical Flecha mission and gives insight into just how orders were executed. As he describes it, in June 1972 at about 1400 hours, when the heat sorely tempted one to siesta, there arrived two Flechas who had left five days earlier on an intelligence-gathering mission near the settlement of Munhango.[25] They looked like local native workers, as they were without uniform and barefoot. Their shirts, worn and faded from an indiscernible original colour, were now varying hues of an earthy brown and were missing several buttons. They were worn outside of the trousers, which likewise were ill-fitting and worn. Unpretentious and wet with perspiration, they entered the modest partitioned offices of PIDE/DGS as if they had just returned from cultivating their fields. Shortly after reporting from their reconnaissance mission, they left without comment to clean up. Despite the heat and their exhaustion, they promptly reappeared in impeccable uniforms in the prefabricated PIDE/DGS office building. They spoke of having had discussions with kinsmen in a settlement north of Munhango, where the day before two armed insurgents had stayed overnight. Afterward, in various conversations with other local people, they learned that an armed group would perhaps, this week, pass to the north in the direction of the southern part of the district of Malange. The account

sounded strange, as there was no report of multiple armed groups in these places; nevertheless, it warranted a reconnaissance patrol.

Believing that it might be an incursion attempting to pass unnoticed, Nogueira e Carvalho made radio contact with the local army sector commander to obtain a 'green light' for an immediate Flecha operation. Next, he called the commander of the Flecha combat group, Comandante Sofrimento, to brief the mission. Like many Africans, he had a single name. He also had a reputation for courage and competence, as he and his men had been successfully entrusted with many missions. Following the calls, the two Flechas left the office without a word.[26]

Meanwhile, Nogueira e Carvalho and his colleagues went about their preparations, devoting particular attention to creating duplicate copies of a rudimentary map of the operational area. The locale was about 36 miles distant, and its approaches were best understood by the local rivers and settlements and by the numerous, distinctive bridges over the water courses. There were ten of these, and all were numbered on the map for reference. Much later these sites and landmarks would be identified with exact coordinates but, for the moment, this simple but effective system worked for the Flechas.[27]

Comandante Sofrimento would personally visit his men after sundown and before the briefing time of 2300, to alert them to the mission and the need to check their arms and equipment thoroughly, as they would be away for a week. A few minutes before the hour, the men began to appear quietly in the briefing rooms, where the PIDE/DGS brigade chief for Bié, other PIDE/DGS agents and Sofrimento were already present. The closed and shuttered window and the smoky lantern created a suffocating atmosphere. The low angle of the light beam projected shadows on the walls and ceiling and lent an eerie appearance to the men's faces, creating a somewhat surreal scene. These men had only a general idea of what they would be doing and no idea of where they would be going, but nothing was questioned. In anticipation there was silence, serious faces and a resolute air. The importance of the briefing was highlighted by the immaculate uniforms and boots shined to a mirror finish, as if there was to be a parade. All stood for the brief and, because of their number, the group overflowed the small office and extended into the two adjoining rooms. At last the entire platoon-sized combat group of 20 Flechas and their commander were present. The briefing was quickly conducted, and afterward all began to relax. The Flechas were issued three combat rations for each day of the mission, ammunition, hand grenades and a radio – the venerable but tried and true TR 28.[28] Sofrimento spoke quietly with his four squad leaders and, following this, the entire combat group began to file slowly from the rooms just as they had entered. The episode in the cramped PIDE/DGS space could not have taken more than 20 minutes from start to finish.[29]

Each of the Flechas left the building alone in the dark, and by indirect routes and irregular timing rendezvoused with Sofrimento at a hut hidden in the elephant grass, perhaps 200 metres away. Between the briefing and departure for the mission

Flechas on patrol in eastern Angola. *Photo Fernando Farinha*

there would be no contact with family or friends, as any careless word could alert the enemy and cost lives. Gossip was not the only danger, as uniquely human scents, such as soap or tobacco, would alert the enemy, and so Sofrimento would check each Flecha for such signs. The Flechas knew that it was important to move silently, to leave no trace and to secure equipment properly so it would make no noise to give them away. Carelessness might provide clues of their presence, such as a flash in the moonlight or an unnatural noise. These would be the mechanical sound of a round being chambered, men's voices in joining up or anything apart from the natural sounds of the night or normal appearances of the day – everything, although it might be a small detail, was very important.[30]

The following morning Nogueira e Carvalho was flown in an old Auster observation aircraft to the first contact point between bridges numbered '6' and '8' and, from a low altitude of about 500 feet, attempted the first scheduled radio contact. Communication was established, and in the midst of the radio conversation the Flechas began taking fire. The radio went silent. Despite many attempts, radio contact remained broken.

Apparently the Flechas had been successful in locating the enemy force but found themselves in a firefight with a reinforced company of UPA/FNLA troops, some 80 to 90 strong. It had come from its Congo base of Kahundu just east of Teixeira de Sousa and infiltrated with the intent of going to the southern part of the district of Malange. Its route had taken it north of Luso next to the Cassai River. The more direct and expected route was across northern Bié, but somehow, inexplicably, the company had made a deviation to the south and crossed into one of the

principal infiltration routes of the MPLA coming from Cassamba in Zambia. It was here that the 20 Flechas encountered the company-sized force.

As they were being attacked, the Flechas broke engagement and split into groups of three. Over the next three days they made their way back via separate routes to Cuemba, the last group arriving at 2000 hours on the third day. There was no loss of equipment, but an irreplaceable Flecha had been killed. Despite the standing order to destroy the radio with a grenade in such cases, the Flechas prided themselves in leaving nothing behind if they had to withdraw. Later that evening, at 2300 hours, the Flechas again, one by one, entered the two small rooms that were the PIDE/DGS office at Cuemba to begin another operation, for such were the Flechas.[31]

Capturing an insurgent leader – almost

Nogueira e Carvalho revealingly describes another Flecha mission that provides insight into the tactics, techniques and procedures employed – this one involved the attempted capture of a high-value target. In the early spring of 1973, there remained isolated pockets of insurgents in the east of Angola; however, they were fairly cut off and their activities were now under relative control. There was an accord with UNITA and restraint on the part of the UPA/FNLA, both undertaken to preserve their organizations in the face of overwhelming military force. Nevertheless, the MPLA and the UPA/FNLA were searching for new fronts and were probing the northeast for weakness. In one instance, a UPA/FNLA group comprised of four men had crossed the border from their Congo base of Kahundu and managed to follow the

Cassai River westward to the area of Alto Chicapa at the southern edge of the district of Lunda. Intelligence on the group came through an informer from a small settlement on their route. The four insurgents, one an important figure, were on their way to meet with additional enemy elements and to provide support and encouragement to this marooned force. According to the informer, they would stay overnight at his settlement on a particular evening. The information was 'close hold', so to speak, and was confined to the informer and the two PIDE/DGS debriefers. It was also highly perishable information; that is, it had to be acted upon quickly or it would be useless. Consequently, the PIDE/DGS post at Luando was alerted to supply a combat group of Flechas to capture these insurgents who were expected to pass

the enemy well. In such an operation, the attacking force would be composed of several small squads of no more than eight men who would easily infiltrate the settlement in the dark without the villagers themselves being aware. This would be done in complete silence – no human voices, no metallic sounds and no exposed shiny objects that might catch and reflect the moonlight. In the half-light of dawn, the attack would be unleashed in a sudden, coordinated move to achieve complete surprise and total disorientation of the villagers and their guests. Time and time again such operations had achieved spectacular results, so much so that General Francisco da Costa Gomes, the Commander-in-Chief of the Armed Forces in Angola, called the Flechas the best soldiers in the world.[34] In this particular case, there would be an

about nine miles to the north of Luando, where the settlement in question was located next to the Cambo River, and where the local tribal chief would play host.[32]

The plan was to surprise the enemy group with a sudden envelopment and capture all four alive. The intelligence to be potentially gleaned from the four and especially from the prominent UPA/FNLA figure, Pedro Afamado, would lead to the capture and neutralization of the isolated insurgents the group was attempting to reach. Pedro Afamado was also a legendary UPA/FNLA commander who had the reputation of being a talented military strategist and leader. In the north of Angola, with access only to limited insurgents and matériel, he had returned again and again, to cause enormous difficulty for the Portuguese.[33] It was the hope of the UPA/FNLA leadership that he could recreate the same success in the east. The insurgents were expected to arrive at the settlement after dark and remain overnight in the tribal chief's hut.

Operations to snatch an important figure or capture a small group were frequently undertaken by Flechas, many of whom were former insurgents themselves and thus understood

Flechas crossing a river in eastern Angola. *Photo Personal archive of Óscar Cardoso*

Flechas crossing the bush in eastern Angola. *Photo Personal archive of Óscar Cardoso*

assault force of eight, with an additional 15 Flechas as a backup or reserve force, making a total of twenty-three. The reserve would remain in the dense bush surrounding the settlement at a standoff of between 50 and 100 metres – a long distance under the circumstances. They would only intervene if needed.[35]

As always, the preparation was very painstaking. When it was dark, the Flechas were called to assemble for a briefing at the PIDE/DGS post, and eight who knew the terrain and the village were selected as the lead squad. All 23 came with their arms and were issued munitions for the mission.[36]

Operational security was vital to a mission of this type, as a tip, however inadvertent, could ruin it all and even result in an unexpected ambush. The informer, for instance, was held in isolation before and during the mission so that he could talk to no one and not be seen by outsiders at the PIDE/DGS post, thereby possibly revealing the intent of the operation. He would not be accompanying the mission, as he would want to remain on good terms with his tribal chief, who was on good terms with both the Portuguese and the enemy. His settlement had never been molested by the insurgents, in spite its being on an enemy penetration route.[37] The community was surviving, something that the Portuguese understood. Likewise, the informer would not be permitted to see the Flechas and possibly recognize them later, something that could endanger them and their families. The Flechas themselves were not permitted any outside contact after being called for a mission. The informal African gossip network is an efficient news wire, and its ability to publish loose talk could easily facilitate the inadvertent passing of delicate information from familial contacts.

With a single exception, each Flecha would carry only his AK-47 rifle, three cartridge clips, a machete and a length of cord. The odd man carried a sawn-off shotgun and five rounds. The commander also took two hand grenades in case they were needed to cover an escape. The AK-47 was the weapon of choice, as it was shorter and more compact than the Heckler & Koch G-3 and hugged the body tightly in a close profile that reduced protrusion and facilitated silent progress through the dense vegetation. No radios were to be taken; normal communication would be by visual signals in daylight and physical touch, sometimes with the aid of a small twig or stick, during darkness. The aim was to move so silently that any noise would be no more than the gentle breeze rustling the grass. When physical contact was lost for any reason, a soft snapping of the fingers was used to request a stop. It was also used to signal danger and thus an immediate stop.

There were designated points for regrouping should any situation develop that required the mission to be aborted or broken for an unexpected development, such as a surprise contact with the enemy or an ambush.[38]

One of the Flechas would wear everyday local clothes in place of a uniform and serve as the point man until the squad was near the settlement, for he knew the trail. He would also approach the outskirts of the settlement and, if he should be seen, he would appear unthreatening and thus unlikely to raise alarm. He would carry the traditional bow and arrow of a Bushman and join the squad after it had passed into the settlement.[39]

As before, the commander checked each man's camouflage dress and tested for the tell-tale smell of soap or other bath products that might give the men away to those who lived permanently in the bush. A local person could detect anything that was not part of their environment. Even the simple smell of toothpaste could be noticed under the proper climatic conditions. Pocket change, wristwatches, wristbands, belts with large bright buckles, sunglasses or any metallic object was to be hidden from view and muffled. Ammunition clips were taped back to back to permit rapid changeover. All three clips as well as the machete were darkened with a charcoal paste and attached to the belt so as to make no noise in moving through the bush.[40]

It was about midnight when the Flechas, one by one at irregular intervals, left the PIDE/DGS post and later regrouped at a point some distance from Luando. This procedure was normal, as extraordinary precautions were necessary with any mission. Such operational security was also important to the survival of the Flechas, as any leak on what they were doing might easily compromise the mission and even result in disaster. Every detail, however trivial, was of major importance.[41]

Once they were assembled and briefed, they departed silently. It was calculated that they would arrive at their objective between 0400 and 0430. At first the bush was easy going, as it was not thick or heavy and the trees were a medium height of perhaps five to ten metres tall. This gave way to a pronounced elevation where the Flechas found it necessary to grab the tree branches to maintain their footing and keep from slipping. It was the *cacimbo*, or drizzle season, a form of winter that occurs between June and October and is characterized by heavy mist and drizzling rain. So everything was wet. The trail had now narrowed to perhaps a foot in width, forcing the Flechas to proceed in single file. Often it simply disappeared into vegetation made lush by weeks of rain. They crossed one small creek after another, all swollen. Most were four or five metres in width and had strong, forceful currents. In one instance, the path crossed a tree trunk that spanned one of the water courses.[42]

The Flecha in mufti led the column by ten to 20 metres. The commander was next, and all followed him so tightly in the inky darkness as if glued to each other. The rearguard trailed the main body of eight slightly. Beginning with the commander, each Flecha extended his arm forward to touch the back of the man ahead of him to avoid stumbling and making any noise should there be a change in pace or direction. The progress of the group was noiseless, even as it deviated from the trail to avoid large trees or thick underbrush. Adjustments to these excursions seemed natural, one man following the next in a seamless and perfectly orchestrated movement.[43]

After about an hour of marching, the rain came. At first there were a few small drops, then larger ones and finally a deluge. The volume of water beating on the group and the surrounding vegetation made an enormous din. Although the downpour lasted only two to three minutes, it seemed like an eternity. It then vanished as quickly as it had appeared, leaving the Flechas soaked and chilled to the bone, but they continued unfazed. After four more hours of walking, the lead Flecha stopped, and the others waited. Word was passed that the group was at the edge of a cassava field belonging to the targeted settlement. After crossing the cultivated field, there would be about 100 metres of bush before the settlement itself. From the earlier briefing in Luando the Flechas knew that there were six thatch-covered huts in the settlement, one of which was large and prominent and located in the centre. This belonged to the tribal chief, and it was here that the important enemy leaders and perhaps 15 to 20 persons were located: this was the objective.[44]

An hour before daybreak, the Flechas separated and began to move into their assault positions. They progressed very, very slowly, each touching the other with his hand for orientation and crouching low in his stealthy approach. All was quiet in the settlement and clearly nothing was expected. By 0445 all were in position, where they waited motionless for the assault hour, only sensing each other in the dark, as the moonlight failed to penetrate the mist. With the lack of movement over time, the chilling early morning dampness had its effect in stiffening their muscles. Gradually the light increased and the outline of the huts became apparent. It was now time to move.[45]

The commander was to enter this main hut with another Flecha after stationing a third outside the entrance to prevent the occupants from fleeing. The others were to be distributed throughout the settlement to prevent any insurgent escape and to control the residents. The reserve waiting beside the cassava field was also alerted. On a signal of two shots fired in the air, the Flechas entered the huts instantaneously. Surprise was total. The chief was alone with two women. In the other huts there were frightened men, women and children. No one yelled but there was much confused talk among the villagers. The Flechas gave orders in a tone that left no doubt about who was in charge, and all obeyed immediately. Only the children cried and a dog barked – a watchdog that had never sensed the presence of the Flechas. The chief was questioned about the enemy, but he knew little other than that they had left earlier. Apparently the enemy travellers had changed their itinerary slightly, which caused the Flechas to miss them.[46] Such is the nature of counterinsurgency, and successes come only with this sort of steady pursuit of the enemy.

Cazombo Salient

Accounts of various Flecha actions stemming from UPA/FNLA and MPLA penetrations of the Cazombo Salient are illustrative of the effectiveness of indigenous troops when they are recruited, trained and motivated to leverage their unique skills against an enemy. There were almost continuous Flecha operations from their founding in 1966 until the end of the war in 1974. Many were unsuccessful in the sense that the ostensible objective was not met, but the constant pressure they exerted on the enemy took its toll on insurgent ability to penetrate eastern Angola with any constructive success. While the Bushmen Flechas operated well in Cuando Cubango, they were not at home beyond there. In Moxico, Lunda and Bié, the Flechas were recruited from local militia and turned former insurgents who, like the Bushmen, knew their areas well and could operate there effectively. These

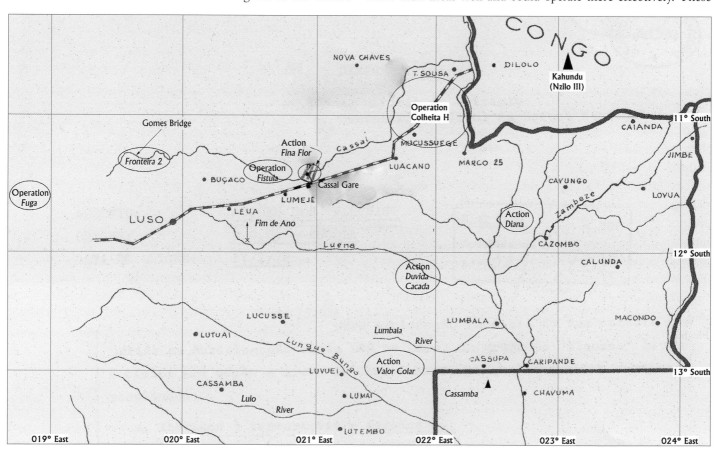

Selected Flecha engagements in the Cazombo Salient, 1970–73. *Map by the author*

newcomers brought slightly different talents in local knowledge and language capabilities, but they were equally as effective when the Bushman-Flecha template was applied. The following accounts of selected Flecha operations against Cazombo Salient penetrations, those coming from the Route of the Cassai (UPA/FNLA) and the Route of the Luena (MPLA), provide an insight to typical successes and disappointments. Over time it is apparent that the Flechas experienced less and less significant contact with the enemy, as the forces of the liberation movements became more and more circumscribed and harried to the point of complete ineffectiveness. The bulk of the action occurred in 1971, as Portuguese forces began to push the enemy farther and farther eastward, tighten the cordon around him, successfully foreclose his offensive, and ultimately restrict his activities to the local frontier buffer.

Operation *Colheita H*, October 1970

In early September, the PIDE/DGS post in Teixeira de Sousa developed intelligence on the UPA/FNLA, indicating that it was concentrating war matériel at its Congo base of Kahundu (Nzilo III) in preparation for infiltration into eastern Angola along the Route of the Cassai. The Congolese authorities were notified in the hope that they would exercise some control over this development; however, they seemed powerless to prevent any intended assault. Further, from 30 September, the UPA/FNLA insurgents began to assemble in significant numbers at Kahundu. Consequently, as a countermeasure, Operation *Colheita H* (Harvest H) was initiated, with two Flecha combat groups from Teixeira de Sousa instructed to intercept the infiltrating enemy, track him and destroy him.[47]

On the evening of 9 November, a group of 30 insurgents crossed the border in the area of the Zanango River, a small tributary of the Luau River, which forms the frontier between Teixeira de Sousa and the Cazombo Salient. According to the Flechas, the group passed through the area of coordinates 10°50'S, 022°11'E at 0515 on 10 December, a month later and only 30 miles from the border, indicating a rather laboured progress. Apparently they were burdened with war matériel and were uncomfortable with the terrain. The Flechas established an ambush site next to the Mucussuege River and just north of the CFB station of that name, a location along the anticipated insurgent route. At 1840 hours on 12 December, they successfully ambushed the intruders, killing six. They also captured three Beretta M951R machine pistols, other war matériel and various documents. The surviving insurgents retired in the direction of the Congo frontier; the Flechas pursued and caught up with them about ten miles northeast of the ambush site. In the ensuing firefight, the Flechas killed two more and captured an old Mauser rifle and other diverse matériel abandoned by the fleeing insurgents.

In an area ten miles north of Mucussuege station, the Flechas captured a lone insurgent who had become separated from the group, and confiscated his Mauser. He was immediately transferred to the PIDE/DGS post at Luacano, where he was interrogated and revealed that the infiltration, of which he was a

Captured weapons. Note 'Flechas' crudely spelled with hand grenades. *Photo Official PIDE/DGS photograph*

General Bettencourt Rodrigues, commander of the Eastern Military Zone in Angola, decorating a Flecha. *Photo Continuidade*

part, had occurred on 9 December around midnight and consisted of 30 enemy elements led by one Julião Coelho, a native of the north of Angola. Their mission was to install themselves north of the Cassai River; however, after crossing the Cassamba River and resting on the banks of the Mucussuege, they were detected by the Flechas and shadowed by helicopter, as they struggled to return to the Congo. Before departing their resting place, they had buried a bazooka with its six grenades, various munitions and a great quantity of hand grenades and Claymore mines. This would create a cache for another incursion, as well as allowing them to flee unburdened and quickly. On 16 December, the Flechas again caught the insurgents crossing the border and fleeing toward Kahundu.[48]

Actions along the Cassai and Luena rivers, December 1970

In early December 1970, during a reconnaissance mission in the area of Umpulo, about 50 miles due south of Cuemba, a Flecha combat group rescued some local Africans from an MPLA column following the Route of the Cuando. One of them was able to provide useful intelligence on the enemy and pinpointed his encampment at the headwaters of the Techissamba River, a small tributary of the important Cuanza River. Coordinates of the camp were reported to be approximately 12°51'30"S, 017°51'E, a position about ten miles southeast of Umpulo and some 250 miles from the eastern border. In the camp were about 50 insurgents, armed with 30 AK-47 assault rifles, two light machine guns, and two rocket-propelled grenades (RPGs).[49] Reconnaissance missions of this sort were organized in areas where there were acknowledged elements of the population lending assistance to the insurgents, forcibly or not. This knowledge was combined with other developing intelligence and known insurgent penetrations, to develop closely defined targeting.

Actions along the Cauela River, December 1970

Based on this reconnaissance, a squad of Flechas was organized and departed for the area on 17 December, with the rescued African, to confirm and further assess the enemy presence. This they did and returned two days later.

From the additional intelligence the Flechas planned an attack predicated on close air support, and the air force was given two days' notice, for it would take the Flechas this length of time to move into position. At the last minute the air force had to cancel its support, as it was the rainy season and flying in such conditions was always tentative. However, the Flechas were now in a position to attack and were committed. Left with no choice but to go ahead without air support, they advanced, successfully assaulting and seizing the enemy camp, destroying and burning it, killing four insurgents, capturing substantial munitions, diverse utensils, various drum magazines for PPSh sub-machine guns and valuable documents.[50] The Flechas suffered one killed and two wounded. The FN rifle belonging to the Flecha casualty was completely destroyed by the direct RPG hit that killed him.[51] The enemy force that fled was subsequently pursued by conventional forces. Had close air support been available, the bulk of the enemy would have been destroyed and the pursuit would have proved less complicated.

Nevertheless, the group was on the defensive, harried deep in Angola and far from support. This penetration represented the western limit of MPLA capability along the Route of the Luena. From this point onward, MPLA forces found the going increasingly difficult.

Twelve days later, on 29 December, a combat group of Flechas operating from Luso as part of Operation *Fim de Ano* (End of Year) detected an enemy encampment belonging to the MPLA. It was located at the headwaters of the Cauela River, a tributary on the left bank of the Luena River in the region of coordinates 11°58'S, 020°35'E, a point about 40 miles due east of Luso. The insurgents, who were penetrating Angola along the Route of the Luena, had abandoned their encampment the day before, leaving its access routes mined with anti-personnel devices and booby traps. Once past these obstacles, the Flechas found 32 huts, which they destroyed after searching them for intelligence.[52]

On leaving the encampment, the Flechas pursued the MPLA column northward by reading the telltale signs along the trail and counted 40 insurgents. The tracks led to an area between the rivers Luauege and Muxixi, where the Flechas were ambushed, suffering one killed and two wounded. In the return fire, the Flechas killed an insurgent and recovered his weapon, an old Soviet Simonov (SKS) 7.62mm calibre.[53] In pursuing the group, the Flechas recovered additional abandoned matériel in the form of an old rifle, some hand grenades, an ammunition box, a can of cooking oil, clothes, various munitions and documents. In addition to the trail of abandoned personal gear, the flight was vividly marked with regular tracks of fresh blood left by the enemy wounded. Following the insurgents became increasingly difficult as they scattered to make their way in smaller groups or individually. Retracing their steps, the Flechas began combing the region of the original contact and pursuit, an area around the lower Luena River, and discovered some eleven abandoned encampments which they destroyed.[54] This Flecha harassing and harrowing of the enemy made his life miserable.

Actions along the Cassai River, February 1971

Two months later, on 14 February at 0600, Flechas from the post at Luso as part of Action *Frontier 2* ambushed an MPLA group of 25 insurgents, as they were in the midst of crossing the Cassai River from the left to the right bank next to the old Gomes Bridge. In this action, the Flechas killed six insurgents, one of whom was a *mestiço*, and recovered the personal arms and munitions of the dead, which included PPSh machine guns, AK-47s and RPGs. Interestingly, the group was led by a fair-complexioned insurgent.[55] Sightings of light-skinned *mestiços* and Europeans in the enemy columns was an indication of the pressure insurgent leaders and Soviet bloc advisers felt to make combat operations successful through their personal presence. Normally neither type took undue risk, and the fact that they were under fire this deep into Angola indicated not only an importance to make good but also a certain distain for Portuguese capabilities.

Actions along the Luando River, February 1971

Barely a week later, between 18 and 22 February, the Flechas from the post at Silva Porto undertook patrols in support of Operation *Fuga* (Flight). During these five days they found and destroyed an encampment of 15 huts located on the left bank of the Luando

River in the region of coordinates 11°42'S, 018°42'E, and another four huts on the right bank of the same river at coordinates 11°41'S, 018°48'E. Both were only recently abandoned. In two huts at the first site there were two hymnals, one in Portuguese and the other in the local Quioco language, soap, salt and a bible. On 20 February, in the vicinity of the two encampments, the Flechas observed two insurgents wearing Portuguese camouflage clothing and armed with the Heckler & Koch G-3 rifles. Unfortunately, they became aware of the Flechas and fled toward the headwaters of the Luambulo River, approximate coordinates 11°48'S, 018°56'E.[56] The insurgents in this area were now without shelter and on the run.

Action along the Lumege and Luqueluque rivers, March 1971

Three weeks later, between 15 and 24 March, during Action *Fístula* (Flute), Flechas from the post at Luso operated between the Lumege and Luqueluque, tributaries on the left bank of the Cassai River, just to the north of Cassai Gare and squarely on the Route of the Cassai. In the course of their patrols, they killed five insurgents and rescued a young girl. They also collected the personal clothing and arms of the dead. In fact, their target was the MPLA political commissar of the Marina Sector, 4th Military Region (IV RM), as he was known to be in the area.[57] Again, the pressure was maintained.

Actions along the Luvua River, July 1971

Later, between 21 and 25 July, a combat group of Flechas as part of Action *Diana* made its way along the left bank of the Luvua River between two of its tributaries, the Calolo and Cambege rivers, in the centre of the Cazombo Salient in search of insurgent penetration. During their progress, the Flechas uncovered and destroyed seven abandoned encampments:

1. Three encampments on the right bank of the Luxiquinha River, about six miles southeast of the village of Lituai. These had been vacated for about 15 days.
2. Two encampments on the left bank of the Luvua River, also abandoned about 15 days previously.
3. Two encampments at the confluence of the Cambege and Luvua rivers, one in a dense thicket situated next to the other, which was composed of about 50 huts. Both had also been abandoned for about 15 days.[58]

Pressure on the enemy and his access to the Cazombo Salient was important, although difficult, as it was quite vulnerable to incursions. Nevertheless, the enemy was never allowed to rest or feel secure.

Actions against the MPLA Section Kangowa, August 1971

In the summer of 1971, PIDE/DGS intelligence sources in Zambia had penetrated the MPLA and revealed that an MPLA column, known as Section *Kangowa*, had been active in Angola and had recruited numerous elements of the population from the border areas to act as porters. These Portuguese nationals were being escorted into Zambia, to the MPLA base of Cassamba, to collect arms, munitions and mines and to bring them into Angola for use by the MPLA.[59]

On 9 August, a short fortnight after Action *Diana*, a combat group of Flechas from Lumbala was briefed and assigned the mission of intercepting this return column, an operation known as Action *Dúvida Caçada* (Doubtful Hunt). On 12 August, on the left bank of the Luena River opposite the mouth of its tributary, the Cafulie River, and near the western border of the Cazombo Salient, the Flechas captured a family of six individuals belonging to an MPLA camp. The prisoners acknowledged that they were part of the group transporting arms and that they had left Zambia on 9 August, three days earlier. They had fallen behind the main group because of the children they were carrying. The head of the family had been forced to join the group at Cassamba to transport armament. The family had anticipated being in Zambia only six days; however, the matériel was not in Cassamba when they arrived, and in this case the group had to wait for it. When they returned to Angola, they travelled at night over two trails that were well known, but the MPLA insurgents had varied the itinerary in an attempt to confuse the porters and prevent them from leading anyone to Cassamba.[60]

Three days later and 30 miles due south, the Flechas detected an ambush on a track that passed next to the Luanguege River at the approximate coordinates of 12°58'S, 021°57'E. It had been set by three insurgents, one armed, coming from Zambia. The Flechas disarmed the one insurgent, taking an old rifle and a pistol from him. The insurgents acknowledged that they were the group leading the porters and reconnoitring a route for resupply. They had also varied the itinerary of the porters to frustrate interception and capture, as well as to protect Cassamba from a raid.[61]

In a separate but related incident, about 12 miles east of Caripande on the southern border of the Cazombo Salient, a captured woman revealed that when the Portuguese had redeployed forces away from Caripande, the MPLA had initiated an intense campaign of radio broadcasts, targeting the local populace, and an immediate expansion of infiltration across the border. One can only wonder at the effectiveness of such broadcasts, as the few locals had neither electricity nor radios. The MPLA had built a camp about 12 miles east of Caripande on the Angolan side of the border and had plans to build another in the vicinity. On further investigation, it appeared that the MPLA was hosting visitors at these three camps, portraying them as an MPLA-occupied portion of Free Angola, to influence international opinion.[62]

Action *Valor Colar*, September 1971

The following month, on 8 September, as a part of Action *Valor Colar* (Gallant Neckless), a combat group of 25 Flechas from the PIDE/DGS post in Lumbala were operating on the western edge of the Cazobmo Salient, when they captured two unarmed insurgents in the vicinity of the MPLA base Março 1. The prisoners were immediately exploited for intelligence and pointed

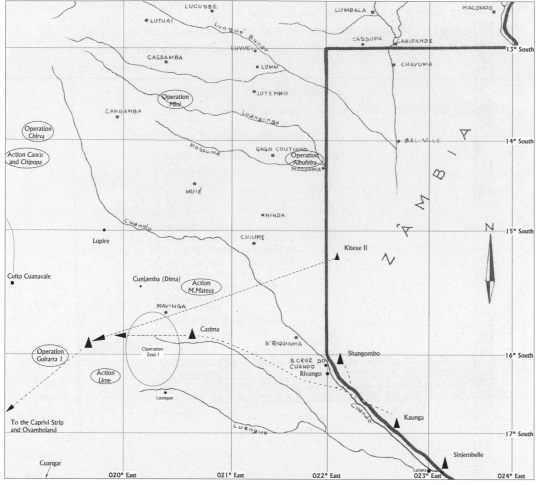

Selected Flecha engagements in Cuando Cubango, 1970–73. *Map by the author*

about 30 miles southeast of their post. They were sprayed with intense enemy fire from bazookas, machine guns and other automatic weapons, in the area of 12°07'S, 020°37'E. In reaction, the Flechas killed an insurgent and recovered his AK-47 and pistol. Again, five miles to the east of the initial contact, the Flechas engaged the enemy and killed another, recovering his weapons and very valuable documentation that he was carrying. The insurgents were wearing uniforms of a new camouflage pattern and used ammunition with abandon, an indication that the logistic chain was flush and that there was much work to be done. The two insurgents killed were identified as 'Orlog' and 'Vietcong', *noms de guerre* for MPLA operatives. 'Orlog' was identified as Manuel Augusto Alfredo, head of the MPLA Department of Logistics and responsible for operations in the 4th Military Region (IV RM).[66] 'Vietcong' was identified as Nobre Manuel Sapi, the political commissar for Squadron *Sakembo*, the ex-Squadron C.[67] Increasingly, enemy leadership was either killed or captured and these losses reduced his capabilities.

to the existence of an MPLA camp in the region of the headwaters of the Caúlo River at the coordinates 13°04'S, 021°38'20"E. At first light on 10 September, the Flechas reached the camp and found it abandoned.[63]

Immediately afterward, in a *chana* about nine miles from the MPLA base of Março 1, the Flechas tracked two large MPLA groups coming from Zambia.[64] They were transporting a great deal of matériel that included bazookas, mortars and many mines of varying types. When the Flechas opened fire over the heads of the group in an attempt to invite surrender, the group returned fire and was immediately supported by its rearguard. After a period of violent combat in which the Flechas expended all their ammunition, the insurgents retreated, leaving six dead and many wounded. One of the wounded, who had a fair complexion and a full beard, was evacuated by the insurgents under covering fire. From the dead and wounded remaining the Flechas took substantial matériel and valuable documents.[65]

The MPLA viewed the easily accessible Cazombo Salient as its own territory and exploited its vulnerability at every opportunity. Initially, it was an insurgent crossroads, and the situation would require almost two years to reverse completely.

Action along the Canage and Luatamba rivers, November 1971

On 27 November 1971, Flechas from the post of Luso engaged an MPLA group in the area between the Canage and Luatamba,

Action just to the north of Cassai Gare, January 1972

On 17 January 1972, Flechas from the post at Luso reacted immediately to reports of MPLA elements operating just north of Cassai Gare, in an operation styled Action *Fina Flor* (Fine Flower). Contact was made with the group, three insurgents were killed and two wounded. Six were captured, among whom was 'Tetembwa', the insurgent João Eduardo Saraiva de Carvalho responsible for reconnaissance and intelligence in the 4th Military Region. He had entered Angola in November 1971. Prior to that he had read two years of law at Coimbra University, from whence he had fled to France in 1968. The weapons and matériel of the killed and captured were retrieved.[68] Maintaining pressure was producing strategic results. In 1972, the routes through and around the Cazombo Salient became quieter and quieter. Neither the UPA/FNLA nor the MPLA was able to mount any truly threatening penetration into Angola, as their abilities to recruit, train and deploy troops with any military skills were being steadily eroded. The area vulnerable to penetration grew smaller by the day, until, by 1973, it was limited to border skirmishes.

Arms captured by the Flechas in eastern Angola.
Photo Personal archive of José Nogueira e Carvalho

A wounded Flecha being evacuated by helicopter in eastern Angola.
Photo Personal archive of Óscar Cardoso

Cuando Cubango

The pattern of harassment continued when the enemy shifted from the Cazombo Salient and sought what he perceived to be an easier route, outflanking Portuguese forces by moving south through Cuando Cubango. This was the home of the Bushmen Flechas and, while early probes through the routes of the Cuando (MPLA) and of the Luio (UNITA) advanced well into the heartland of Angola, as far as Bié and Malange, such overextension made these penetrations extremely vulnerable and isolated. The insurgents were now experiencing their culminating points, with long, insecure logistic lines of communication reaching all the way back into Zambia.

Actions along the Cuito River, December 1970

Between 10 and 20 December, Flechas from the post of Cuito Cuanavale took part in the Action *Caucu*, targeting penetrations 200 miles west of the Zambian frontier along the Route of the Cuando. In the course of this action they destroyed the following MPLA encampments:

1. Nhamalanda at the approximate coordinates 13°57'S, 018°27'E
2. Cafute at the approximate coordinates 14°04'S, 018°38'E
3. Luela at the approximate coordinates 13°58'S, 018°43' E

4. Two deactivated encampments in the area of the Cutima and Longa Norte rivers, tributaries on the right bank of the Cuito River.

During the operation five insurgents were killed, four of whom were known leaders. In addition to rescuing a woman, a substantial amount of abandoned weapons and matériel was recovered.[69]

Actions along the Mussuma River, February 1971

Two months later, during the period from 12 to 15 February, a group of 40 Flechas from the PIDE/DGS post at Gago Coutinho participated in Operation *Albufeira* (Lagoon), which was in response to the broad incursions along the Route of the Cuando by MPLA forces. The Flechas were deployed along the left bank of the Mussuma River, between the frontier post of that name and the mouth of the Cafuto River, a distance of about eight miles, and north from this east–west axis to the headwaters of the Cafuto, a distance of about six miles. On the left bank of the Cafuto, in the region of the approximate coordinates 14°06'S, 021°46'E, the Flechas found and destroyed an enemy encampment that, from all indications, had been abandoned in haste only moments earlier. Shortly afterward, as the Flechas picked up the direction of flight and began an eastward pursuit, they were ambushed ineffectively by the enemy rearguard with automatic weapons and two RPG rounds. The Flechas returned fire, killing three MPLA troops and wounding an unknown number of others, who left traces of blood on the ground as they fled. The MPLA column continued its retreat eastward to the frontier and the sanctuary of Zambia, only some 22 miles distant, as the Flechas pursued them all the way to the border, maintaining pressure. From footprints the Flechas calculated the force to number about 70 insurgents.[70]

Action along the Route of the Luanguinga (MPLA), July 1971

In the course of supporting Operation *Mini*, the Flechas assaulted an MPLA encampment on the banks of the Toqueque River at the approximate coordinates of 13°29'S, 020°29'E, where part of the Squadron *Angola Livre* (Free Angola) was headquartered. The encampment had been abandoned some days earlier and a number of its huts destroyed by the departing insurgents. Its layout contained an enclosure appropriate for briefings and political indoctrination, as well as for drill instruction or parades. A local settlement was close by the abandoned installation and had been exploited for local support.[71] Various groups of Flechas who habitually operated in the region were familiar with the area between the rivers Luanguinga and Luio and knew the Toqueque River as a tributary of the former. They had not previously seen insurgents in this area.

Meanwhile, an African, by the name of Benate Chiloa, presented himself at Cassamba, about 30 miles due north of the action, and related the following story. He had been kidnapped by the insurgents about two months before and taken to an MPLA encampment on the Toqueque River that belonged to *Angola Livre* and where he was given instruction by the insurgent

Codinguinda. On 30 July, during the confusion generated by a contact with Flechas, he escaped and came to the authorities. Within the encampment he had seen three 60mm mortars, one 82mm mortar, two bazookas, four machine guns with bipods and various other automatic weapons and hand grenades. There were about 50 insurgents, of whom there were five leaders: 'Fogo', 'Quase', 'Chimbuambua', 'Diamante' (Luïs Vasco Kapenda, commander of Zone D, III RM), and 'Pacaça', all *noms de guerre*. The camp was located at the approximate coordinates of 13°16'S, 019°54'E, in an area of thick grass and no huts.[72] During Chiloa's stay with *Angola Livre*, he had been forced to listen to speeches by the political commissar Catema, who denigrated UNITA as a movement that did not engage the people and, at the same time, exalted the MPLA as the movement with the capacity and vision to liberate Angola. In a meeting of the five MPLA commanders, they resolved to open the road to Cuemba, where there were thought to be elements of UNITA with whom they could join forces. In fact, Portuguese intelligence was to the contrary: the true mission of *Angola Livre* was to annihilate UNITA along the Route of the Luanguinga and attack its local refuges with the objective of 'cleansing the area' so that the MPLA would have a better penetration of Bié.[73] This reflected the competition between the independence movements that would eventually result in UNITA coming to terms with the Portuguese and agreeing to limit its armed action to fighting the MPLA.

Actions along the Lunhonde River, August 1971

A month later, on 7 August, there were 50 Flechas from the PIDE/DGS post at Serpa Pinto participating in Operation *Chirva* (Goat), whose purpose was to reconnoitre a group of MPLA insurgents calculated to number two hundred. The Flechas easily located the group on the left bank of the Lunhonde River, at the approximate coordinates of 14°02'S, 018°52'E. This particular group of insurgents had demonstrated an elevated level of effectiveness in finding their way 200 miles into Angola from Zambia along the Route of the Cuando. This 'squadron', as they called themselves, had crossed the border in the south of the area opposite Gago Coutinho and entered MPLA Zones D and F of its 3rd Military Region (III RM). Intelligence indicated that their destination was the 6th Military Region (VI RM), where they would proselytize the population.[74] Further, the Flechas destroyed four MPLA encampments, killed four insurgents and rescued 16 men, 47 women and 56 children from the local population impressed into working for the MPLA. Incidental matériel abandoned in flight was recovered.[75]

In this encounter the MPLA squadron sensed that it outnumbered the Flechas and began to encircle them. The Flechas opened with intense fire from mortars and bazookas and frustrated the intentions of the squadron, which was forced to withdraw to the east in the direction of the Tempué River. The Flechas recovered a small number of enemy arms abandoned in flight.[76] The MPLA column became the target of Operation *Siroco*, a major military offensive.[77]

Action along the Uasseque and Uanhomba vivers, August 1971

The presence of this MPLA squadron so far in the interior and in such numbers showed advanced MPLA capability and portended increasing support for SWAPO. At the same time, in the south, large groups were attempting to penetrate similar distances from the Zambian MPLA bases, Shangombo, Kaunga and Sinjembelle, in order to bring SWAPO insurgents across southern Angola and help them infiltrate the Caprivi Strip and Ovamboland, border areas of South West Africa. SWAPO advocated the independence of South West Africa and was fighting South African forces in an insurgency there. From Zambia the most direct route to South West Africa was across southern Angola.

MPLA Squadron *Cuidado* had initially opened this way across the area and guided elements of SWAPO from Zambia to the region of the Cuamato people next to the Cunene River and the frontier with the South African area of Ovamboland. Here, there was much cross-border sympathy among the local people, which made the transit across the border easy for SWAPO insurgents. Transit of SWAPO forces, supported by the MPLA, was to become an increasing security problem in Cuando Cubango and Huíla, as transit routes developed across these largely empty districts where intruders were likely to be unchallenged by Portuguese security forces.[78] Flecha pressure on the enemy in the south would intensify and make the seemingly wide open and benign routes dangerous for the interlopers.

Later the same month, between 17 August and 2 September, a combat group of 25 Flechas from the post of Cuangar participated in Action *Ume* (Alum), which was aimed at clearing the headwaters of the Uasseque (Uaséque) and Uanhomba rivers, where it was thought that an MPLA/SWAPO group was transiting from Zambia to Ovamboland. The Flechas concentrated their patrolling along the Gueche River, located between the two larger rivers and in an area about 100 miles northeast of Cuangar. At about 0700 on 30 August, they detected an MPLA encampment on the left bank of the Uanhomba, at approximately 16°23'S, 019°40'E. During the attack, which lasted five hours, the Flechas were unable to dislodge the enemy because of his superior numbers and elevated ability to return fire. With their ammunition exhausted, they were forced to disengage. The insurgents suffered four dead and one wounded. The Flechas noticed that among the insurgents there were many from the Vassequele people, an ethnic minority who were known to be oppressed by other Africans in Cuando Cubango. That the MPLA had recruited these outcasts was evidence that the enemy group had lost its way and needed local guides into the Angolan interior.[79]

Intercepts of insurgents, September 1971

MPLA infiltration in August prompted a wider effort to intercept matériel entering Angola from Zambia, and Flecha detachments were mobilized to this effect.[80] Between 6 and 10 September, Flechas from the PIDE/DGS post at Mavinga were operating along the left bank of the Lomba River in Action *M. Mateus*, when they intercepted a group of seven MPLA porters at the

A Flecha in pursuit of the enemy, near Ninda in eastern Angola.
Photo Fernando Farinha

Flechas in pursuit of the enemy, near Ninda in eastern Angola.
Photo Fernando Farinha

approximate coordinates of 15°37'S, 020°37'E, just northeast of Mavinga. When the seven attempted to flee, the Flechas shot and killed one of them, Fulai Pedro. The group originated from the MPLA base of Sikongo (Kitexe II) in Zambia and was on its way to the MPLA encampment of Cazima, located about 90 miles due west of Rivungo on the right bank of the Capembe River. The Flechas took possession of some personal munitions and a large supply of uniforms: 49 pairs of trousers, 40 shirts and 30 berets, all made in a camouflage identical to that of the Portuguese.[81]

Later, between 16 August and 11 September, the Flechas from the PIDE/DGS post at Cuito Cuanavale, in support of Action *Candongo*, apprehended two MPLA insurgents, five women and four children near the settlement of Lupire. The men were carrying ammunition pouches with 9mm cartridges, but no weapons.[82]

On 12 September, again Flechas from Cuito Cunavale in support of Action *Chipopa* assaulted an MPLA camp on the right bank of the Cuito River at the approximate coordinates of 14°10'S, 018°48'E, killing two insurgents and capturing their personal arms, ammunition and valuable documents. A little over a mile from the camp the Flechas detected an anti-personnel mine that exploded the moment it was raised, apparently booby-trapped against countermeasures. One of the Flechas was gravely wounded in the explosion.[83]

Action along the Lunga, Cuveli, and Cuito Rivers, June 1973

Between 13 and 19 June, a group of Flechas from the post at Catota as part of Operation *Guitarra 1* (Guitar 1) combed the area of the left bank of the Cuvelai between its confluences with the Longa and Cuito rivers. During a week of continuous patrolling, the Flechas rescued two men, three women and three children.[84] Things had become relatively quiet.

From this point, action after action yielded fewer and fewer results. The MPLA proved incapable of making any sustained penetration of southeastern Angola and, while there was conflict along the border, the interior became quiet, free of insurgents, and relatively secure.

Dembos region

The north of Angola had always presented a tempting target for insurgents, as it was the most direct route to Luanda, the perceived centre of gravity for the Portuguese. Despite its appeal, it was a difficult route, as the terrain was forbidding. This situation worked both ways, as the insurgents were able to hide easily in the jungle mountains of the Dembos but could not easily mount offensives from their redoubts.

On the other hand, the Portuguese could limit the enemy to his fastness. The answer to routing him from his sanctuary was through the use of the Flechas, in combination with heavier

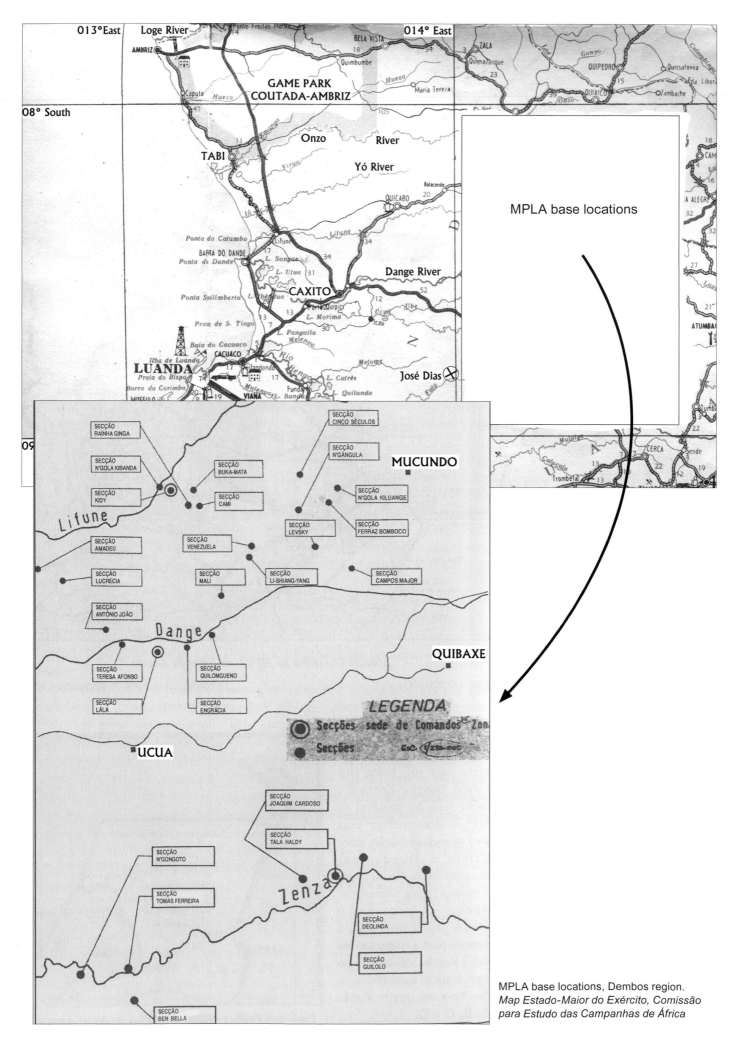

MPLA base locations, Dembos region.
Map Estado-Maior do Exército, Comissão para Estudo das Campanhas de África

ground forces and air support. In the north Flechas were locally recruited Africans and turned insurgents who had been through the Flecha training course. Their operations in this sector parallel those in the east and were most effective.

Encampment José Dias, March 1971

In one of the few effective reappearances of UPA/FNLA insurgents in the Dembos area, a new column appeared in March 1971 and established a base camp named José Dias, in honour of one of its luminaries. This camp was well defended and quickly became the source of much mischief. The Flechas, operating in the area, on 7 March, identified the encampment at coordinates 08°49'S, 013°58'E and laid plans to assault it the next day. At about 0430 hours, just prior to dawn, when the Flechas were encircling the headquarters, they were taken under fire by the insurgents. In the ensuing action, the Flechas rescued two men, six women and eleven children and took a *canhangulo*. In debriefing the rescued group, the Flechas learned that the insurgents maintained a rigorous lookout, as every evening the area was subject to aerial reconnaissance.[85] Now located, its further prosecution was given over to heavier forces.

Caxito, February 1972–July 1973

Nearly a year later, on 13 February, a letter was received at the PIDE/DGS post of Caxito, written by a pioneer or young recruit of the MPLA, Alfredo Muginga, who was the brother of a Flecha operating from there. It alerted the post that he was with a group of insurgents at coordinates 08°37'S, 014°02'E who wished to surrender and were fleeing control of the MPLA. A combat group of Flechas was dispatched to the area and rescued ten insurgents, two pioneers and two women from the encampment known as Teresa Afonso, named for an MPLA battlefield heroine.[86] This contact prompted Action *Titilar* (Tickle) in the difficult area east of Caxito, with the intent of cleansing it of insurgents. The insurgents and their encampments were scattered and well hidden, but the action of the Flechas kept them on the move and provided no respite. When *Titilar* ended on 25 March, the Flechas had killed four insurgents, captured one and recovered their personal arms. Likewise, they had rescued two men, eight women and seven children, and destroyed two encampments.[87] Clearly the work was not completed in this area and follow-up operations were needed. These took the form of the *Kiabixila* series of actions.

Two days later, in Action *Kiabixila-2*, the Flechas located, attacked and destroyed the MPLA Section *Lálá*, which was the command centre of its Military Region I (I RM). In this action three insurgents were killed, two captured and various wounded. Two men and two children were rescued, and the personal arms and matériel of the killed and captured were recovered. At the height of the action, the Flechas managed to detonate a mine without consequence. Afterward, when they were pursuing the insurgent commander and coordinator of Military Region I, José César Augusto, known as 'Kiluanje', they came under heavy fire from a Soviet Degtyaryov DP-28 light machine gun as they were crossing the Dange River.[88] The canoe containing the Flechas capsized, spilling them into the water, and one lost his arm from wounds in the mêlée. The insurgent fire was silenced by those Flechas on the opposite bank waiting to cross, while those in the water were being rescued, particularly the two who were in difficulty from their wounds. There were no Flechas lost in the action.[89]

In the final days of March, the post at Caxito received intelligence that a group of MPLA insurgents were at 08°31'40"S, 013°50'30"E, and so, on the evening of 29 March, a group of Flechas departed on a reconnaissance mission. In the course of their patrol, they captured the following MPLA leadership:[90]

1. Abílio Sebastião Francisco, variously Agostinho Sebastião Francisco, 'Folhas Caídas', Chief of Section *Engrácia*
2. Castro André, 'Não Contava', insurgent in Section *Engrácia*[91]
3. Manuel António Policarpo, 'Por Si', Group Chief in Section *Engrácia*
4. José Domingos, 'Kuata Coco', member of Action Group, Section *Tala Hady*[92]
5. Domingos Pedro José, 'Kiba Kia Tele', Chief of Action Group, Section *Joaquim Cardoso*[93]

Between 31 March and 3 April, two groups of Flechas, also operating from Caxito, supported Action *Kiabixila-3* in which the MPLA sections *Engrácia*, *Lucrécia*, *Teresa Afonso* and *Lálá* were destroyed.[94] During the fighting, four insurgents were captured and five children rescued.[95]

A year later, between 16 and 19 June 1973, Flechas from Caxito participated in Action *Kihumbi-8*, investigating the area around the Yó River, where they killed the MPLA insurgents Manuel Mugunga Mateus, Mateus Muginga and Videira António from Company *Gibóia* (Boa Constrictor), rescued three women and two children, and recovered the personal arms of those killed.[96]

Following on from this success, the Flechas detected and followed the tracks of a group of 25 insurgents moving southeast in the direction of Terra Nova, a village in the mountain vastness of the Dembos, just east of Malanje. Here the insurgents made a judgment error and suffered three wounded. They subsequently fled, abandoning some salt and bananas and parts of Claymore mines.[97] This was a group attempting to resupply Company *Gibóia*, which was subsisting exclusively on meat from hunting, a situation similar to that of Company *Tigre* (Tiger) operating in the area of Tabi, a small coastal village about 40 miles north of Luanda and bordering the game park Coutada-Ambriz.

A week later, between 24 and 28 June 1973, the Flechas from Caxito supported Action *Kihumbi-9*, in which they captured an MPLA leader and an insurgent and their personal arms at 08°08'50"S, 013°33'40"E, a position 20 miles due north of Caxito and just across the Yó Rover. The leader was Sebastião Mabiala Paulo, the sub-commander with the UPA/FNLA and chief of the Platoon *TNT* of Company *Dimuca*. The Flechas were also taken

Flechas prepare to board a helicopter after many days in the field. *Photo Fernando Farinha*

under fire with bursts from a Sterling sub-machine gun, without effect, while rescuing a woman and finding 20 9mm rounds that the MPLA had dropped.[98]

The next week, between 3 and 7 July, the Flechas from Caxito, while participating in Action *Kihumbi-10*, found two abandoned MPLA encampments at coordinates 08°14'15"S, 013°48'50"E and 08°15'20"S, 013°44'20"E. During the same period the Flechas participating in *Kihumbi-12* detected an MPLA encampment in the region of 08°19'S, 013°36'30"E, where they rescued Bernardo Milagre. He had been impressed into Platoon No. 1 (*Banza Bungo*) of Company *Gibóia* about two years earlier.[99]

Also during this period additional Flechas from Caxito, participating in Action *Kussota*, assaulted Company *Dimuka* in the early hours of 6 July, killing three insurgents and wounding three others. Among the dead was Manuel Sebastião Júnior, 'Diviluka', who commanded the company and was the deputy commander for Front No. 1 of the UPA/FNLA. The encampments of the 2nd and 3rd platoons of the company were located but found abandoned.[100]

In these actions the Flechas noticed and reported symptoms of indiscipline, disorganization and demoralization among the UPA/FNLA troops operating in Front No. 1, in the area between the Loge and Onzo rivers, which define the northern and southern boundaries of the Coutada-Ambriz. Captured documents indicated that a total of 667 'military' personnel had returned to the Congo since December 1971 and were part of the clandestine dissident activity in the UPA/FNLA camp at Kinkuzu. Apparently

in this case there was a complete failure of the political commissars to maintain troop loyalty to the Holden Roberto regime.[101]

On departing their operational area, the Flechas were taken under fire without consequence. The next day as they approached the pick-up point, they were again taken under fire and returned it, killing an insurgent and capturing Sebastião Francisco António from the 1st Platoon, Company *Dimuka*. One of the captured-wounded was Simão Timótec Alberto, 'Vasoura', commander of Company *Vasoura*. He later died of his wounds.[102]

Again, a week later, between 10 and 13 July, Flechas from Caxito, during *Kihumbi-13*, captured two UPA/FNLA insurgents, João Francisco Nicolau and João Pedro Maningo, and rescued two men, seven women and nine children. In later action they killed João Sebastião. These various actions involved insurgents from Company *Tigre*, whose members were surviving like nomads and had been dispersed as a result of Flecha action. The company commander, Paulo Sebastião Domingos, 'São Paulo', was on the run and hiding in the bush with his fellow insurgent, Mateus Dias Ideia. They were now using their weapons and precious little remaining ammunition to survive by hunting game rather than fighting.[103]

Catete, June–July 1973

Catete, located some 35 miles due south of Catexe, was likewise in an area of rivers and forests that favoured the insurgent. By this late in the war, their effectiveness here was also considerably diminished when compared with earlier experiences and, increasingly, those captured were in desperate condition and simply surviving in the bush and forests. While they posed a threat, it was insubstantial. The Flechas, who felt quite comfortable operating in the bush and forests, were patiently tracking the insurgents and either killing or capturing them. Between 19 and 23 June, in Action *Aço Rico* (Solid Steel), the Flechas captured an MPLA insurgent, Domingos Sebastião, 'Devagar', and rescued five men, six women and ten children. Later the same day they captured two more MPLA insurgents, Simão Bernardo Miguel, 'Verdade', and Manuel João António, 'Herói', and rescued a man, two women and two children, all from Section *Ben Bella*.[104]

Later between 2 and 4 July, the Flechas from Catete participated in Action *Ana Rosa*, in which they captured five MPLA insurgents, the most significant being Isaac Domingues, 'Leste de Angola', ex-'Franco', the political commissar. All of these belonged to the former Section *Ben Bella* and were attempting to lay the ground work for the arrival of Moises Micolo, 'Tété dos Tombos', who was to resuscitate the MPLA influence in the area through *'lumpenismo'* – presumably a method of leveraging the underclass to gain victory.

During Action *Ana Rita* between 9 and 13 July, the Flechas, again from Catete, captured five MPLA insurgents, two of whom were political officers, and rescued a man, 15 women, seven pioneers and twenty children. A bit later, they killed five insurgents, rescued nine women, one pioneer and ten children. These insurgents belonged to the MPLA Section *Ben Bella* and like many others were living as nomads. The group was surviving next to the Base *Tomás Ferreira*, which the Flechas had destroyed earlier on 17 June.[105] Most of the insurgent troops had returned to the Congo, now known as Zaïre, and those remaining were psychologically spent from the relentless pressure of the Flechas and other Portuguese forces. Section after section had been dissolved, and those responsible ordered the remaining to live near native villages for support. This facilitated their capture and the rescue of those elements of the population forced to support them.[106]

The success of constant pressure

In the north of Angola, by the end of the war, both the UPA/FNLA and the MPLA were forces strangled and without vigour, confined to a completely circumscribed area in the fastness of the Dembos region. Both were isolated, starving, only partially armed and desperate. The Dembos was difficult for anyone because of its impossible terrain; in essence, hiding there, as the enemy forces were doing, was neutralizing oneself as a threat.

In the east of Angola, the UPA/FNLA and the MPLA were destroyed. For the UPA/FNLA the crisis was complete. For the MPLA, it was reduced to sneaking across the border from its bases in Zambia and planting mines along the frontier roads. Its actions along the border were violent and short in both duration and penetration. The notion here was to strike a blow against the Portuguese that would open the way for a column to penetrate inland. This never worked. In the opinion of Brigadier Hélio Felgas, commander of the Eastern Sector, by the beginning of April 1974 there was no contact between Portuguese forces and the insurgent groups of any of the nationalist organizations. By the end of April the southeast of Angola was calm, with insurgent activity practically nonexistent.[107]

The relentless pursuit of the enemy on both the northern and eastern fronts militarily defeated him; indeed, the Flechas at one stage accounted for 60 per cent of all enemy kills and won the admiration of General Costa Gomes, the Commander-in-Chief of the Armed Forces in Angola.[108] While this offensive was the result of a united effort by all elements of the Portuguese Armed Forces, the Flechas played a successful and unique role, so much so that its duplication in other theatres and other wars was attempted but never with quite the success of Angola.

1   Ibid, p. 24.

2   Ibid, p. 25

3   Ibid.

4   Comissão para o Estudo das Campanhas de África, *Resenha Histórico-Militar das Campanhas de África 1961–1974, 6 Volume, Aspectos da Actividade Operacional, Tomo I, Angola–Livro 2* [Historical Military Report on the African Campaigns 1961–1974, 6 Volume, Aspects of Operational Activity, Tome I, Angola, Book 2] (Lisbon: Estado-Maior de Exército, 2006), pp. 223-8.

5   Ibid, p. 25.

6   Adelino Gomes, 'Exército e UNITA Colaboraram antes de 74' [Army and UNITA Collaborate before 74], *Público* (19 December 1995), pp. 2-4; and Óscar Cardoso, 'Criador dos Flech' [Creator of the Flechas] in José Freire Antunes, *A Guerra de África, 1961–1974, Volume 1* [The War in Africa, 1961–1974, Volume 1] (Lisbon: Temas e Debates, 1996), pp. 409-10.

7   Dalila Cabrita Mateus, *A PIDE/DGS na Guerra Colonial 1961–1974* [The PIDE/DGS in the Colonial War 1961–1974] (Lisbon: Terramar, 2004), pp. 199-207.

8   Pires Nunes, p. 19.

9   Ibid, inside front cover; and João Paulo Borges Coelho, 'African Troops in the Portuguese Colonial Army, 1961–1974: Angola, Guinea-Bissau and Mozambique,' *Portuguese Studies Review* (Spring–Summer 2002), pp. 129-50.

10 Ibid, p. 67.

11 John P. Cann, *Contra-Subversão em África* [Counterinsurgency in Africa] (Lisbon: Prefácio, 2005), p. 30.

12 Pires Nunes, p. 40.

13 Ibid.

14 Comissão para o Estudo das Campanhas de África, *Resenha Histórico-Militar das Campanhas de África 1961–1974*, p. 353.

15 Ibid.

16 Ibid.

17 Pires Nunes, p. 42.

18 Comissão para o Estudo das Campanhas de África, *Resenha Histórico-Militar das Campanhas de África 1961–1974*, pp. 352-71.

19 Ibid, p. 356.

20 Direcção Geral de Segurança, '*Relatório de Interpretação de Documentos Apreendidos pelos Flechas na Acção "Flecha 2" Relativo à Logística'* [Report of Interpretation of Documents Taken by the Flechas of the Subdelegation of this DGS in Luso in the Operation "Flecha 2" Pertaining to Logistics], Nº 12/71-DINF-2ª, 13 December 1971, SDGN 1802, report 12/71, Arquivo da Defesa Nacional, Paço do Arcos, Portugal, p. 13.

21 Ibid.

22 Ibid.

23 Renato F. Marques Pinto, correspondence with the author, 9 August 1995.

24 Peter Stiff, *The Covert War: Koevoet Operations 1979–1989* (Alberton, South Africa: Galago Books, 2004), p. 69.

25 José Nogueira e Carvalho, *Era Tempo de Morrer em África: Angola, Guerra e Decolonização, 1961–1975* [It Was a Time of Death in Africa: Angola, War and Decolonization, 1961–1975] (Lisbon: Prefácio, 2004), p. 184.

26 Ibid.

27 Ibid.

28 The Racal TR 28 was a 25-watt, single side band (SSB), AM HF, crystal-

controlled backpack radio manufactured in South Africa.

29 Nogueira e Carvalho, p. 185.

30 Ibid, pp. 185-6.

31 Ibid, p. 188.

32 Ibid, p. 190.

33 Fernando Rocha, 'Guerra de Angola/Vale do Loge, Toto e Faz' [Angolan War/ Loge Valley, Toto and Faz], *Mistura Grossa* [Large Mixture], 18 August 2010, http://www.misturagrossa.net/?p=1402 (accessed 23 March 2013).

34 Nogueira e Carvalho, p. 192.

35 Ibid.

36 Ibid, p. 193.

37 Ibid, p. 192.

38 Ibid, p. 194.

39 Ibid.

40 Ibid.

41 Ibid.

42 Ibid, p. 195.

43 Ibid.

44 Ibid, p. 196.

45 Ibid.

46 Ibid, pp. 197-8.

47 IAN/TT, Arquivos de PIDE, Torre do Tombo, Lisbon, Processo 7477-CI(2), Operações Diversas, pasta 33, 6, 7, and 8.

48 Ibid.

49 Direcção Geral de Segurança, '*Acções das Nossas Forces*' [Actions of Our Forces], DGS-Angola, 23 December 1970, SDGN 1802, Intelligence Report 14, Arquivo da Defesa Nacional, Paço do Arcos, Portugal.

50 The PPSh-41 (*Pistolet-Pulemet Shpagina*, from the Russian, and *41* from the 1941 date of manufacture) was the result of two national catastrophes for the Soviet Union. The first was the Winter War with Finland in 1939–40 when the Finns used sub-machine guns with devastating effect during close combat in the forests, and the second was the German invasion of 1941 when the Soviets lost in the retreats both huge quantities of small arms and much of their engineering capability. There then arose an urgent demand for a light and simple weapon capable of a high volume of fire, and the answer to this was the PPSh-41, designed by Georgii Shpagin. It was much cheaper and quicker to make than the preceding models and was finished roughly. The barrel was still chromed, however, and there was never any doubt about its effectiveness. About five million PPSh guns had been made by 1945, and the Soviets adapted their infantry tactics to take full advantage of such huge numbers. In the Soviet Union, the PPSh went out of service in the late 1950s, but it has been supplied in enormous quantities to Soviet satellite and pro-communist countries, so that it will be seen for many years.

51 Ibid.

52 Direcção Geral de Segurança, '*Acções das Nossas Forces*' [Actions of Our Forces], DGS-Angola, 4 January 1971, SDGN 1802, Intelligence Report 49, Arquivo da Defesa Nacional, Paço do Arcos, Portugal.

53 The SKS is a Soviet semi-automatic rifle chambered for the 7.62x39mm round, designed in 1943 by Sergei Gavrilovich Simonov. Its complete designation, SKS-45, is an abbreviation for Selfloading Karbine Simonov 1945. In the early 1950s, the AK-47 replaced it. Because 15 million were produced, it has been supplied in generous quantities to Soviet satellite and pro-communist countries and to liberation movements. So, like the PPSh, it will be seen for many years.

54 Ibid.

55 Direcção Geral de Segurança, '*Acções das Nossas Forces*' [Actions of Our Forces], DGS-Angola, 16 February 1971, SDGN 1802, Intelligence Report 203, Arquivo da Defesa Nacional, Paço do Arcos, Portugal.

56 Direcção Geral de Segurança, '*Acções das Nossas Forces*' [Actions of Our Forces], DGS-Angola, 25 February 1971, SDGN 1802, Intelligence Report 249, Arquivo da Defesa Nacional, Paço do Arcos, Portugal.

57 Direcção Geral de Segurança, '*Acções das Nossas Forces*' [Actions of Our Forces], DGS-Angola, 26 March 1971, SDGN 1802, Intelligence Report 356, Arquivo da Defesa Nacional, Paço do Arcos, Portugal.

58 Direcção Geral de Segurança, '*Acções das Nossas Forces*' [Actions of Our Forces], DGS-Angola, 11 August 1971, SDGN 1802, Intelligence Report 947, Arquivo da Defesa Nacional, Paço do Arcos, Portugal.

59 Direcção Geral de Segurança, '*Acções das Nossas Forces*' [Actions of Our Forces], DGS-Angola, 17 August 1971, SDGN 1802, Intelligence Report 963, Arquivo da Defesa Nacional, Paço do Arcos, Portugal.

60 Ibid.

61 Ibid.

62 Direcção Geral de Segurança, '*Acções das Nossas Forces*' [Actions of Our Forces], DGS-Angola, 23 August 1971, SDGN 1802, Intelligence Report 976, Arquivo da Defesa Nacional, Paço do Arcos, Portugal.

63 Direcção Geral de Segurança, '*Acções das Nossas Forces*' [Actions of Our Forces], DGS-Angola, 14 September 1971, SDGN 1802, Intelligence Report 1069, Arquivo da Defesa Nacional, Paço do Arcos, Portugal.

64 A *chana*, *xana*, or *anhara* is an Angolan (Umbundo) term that refers to flat, plain-like country with very low vegetation, normally grass. When *chanas* are crossed by rivers, they are frequently inundated, particularly in the rainy season.

65 Direcção Geral de Segurança, '*Acções das Nossas Forces*' [Actions of Our Forces], DGS-Angola, 14 September 1971, SDGN 1802, Intelligence Report 1069, Arquivo da Defesa Nacional, Paço do Arcos, Portugal.

66 Direcção Geral de Segurança, '*Relarório de Interpretação de Documentos Apreendios pelos Flechas na Acção "Flecha 2" Relativo à Logística*' [Report of Interpretation of Documents Taken by the Flechas of the Subdelegation of this DGS in Luso in the Operation "Flecha 2" Pertaining to Logistics], Nº 12/71-DINF-2ª, 13 December 1971, SDGN 1802, report 12/71, Arquivo da Defesa Nacional, Paço do Arcos, Portugal, 4; and Direcção Geral de Segurança, '*Acções das Nossas Forces*' [Actions of Our Forces], DGS-Angola, 30 November 1971, SDGN 1802, Intelligence Report 1400, Arquivo da Defesa Nacional, Paço do Arcos, Portugal.

67 Ibid.

68 Direcção Geral de Segurança, '*Acções das Nossas Forces*' [Actions of Our Forces], DGS-Angola, 17 January 1972, SDGN 1802, Intelligence Report 99, Arquivo da Defesa Nacional, Paço do Arcos, Portugal.

69 Direcção Geral de Segurança, '*Acções das Nossas Forces*' [Actions of Our Forces], DGS-Angola, 7 January 1971, SDGN 1802, Intelligence Report 49, Arquivo da Defesa Nacional, Paço do Arcos, Portugal.

70 Direcção Geral de Segurança, '*Acções das Nossas Forces*' [Actions of Our Forces], DGS-Angola, 13 February 1971, SDGN 1802, Intelligence Report 203, Arquivo da Defesa Nacional, Paço do Arcos, Portugal.

71 Direcção Geral de Segurança, '*Acções das Nossas Forces*' [Actions of Our Forces], DGS-Angola, 14 August 1971, SDGN 1802, Intelligence Report 963, Arquivo da Defesa Nacional, Paço do Arcos, Portugal.

72 Ibid.

73 Ibid.

74 Direcção Geral de Segurança, '*Acções das Nossas Forces*' Forces [Actions of Our Forces], DGS-Angola, 11 August 1971, SDGN 1802, Intelligence Report 947, Arquivo da Defesa Nacional, Paço do Arcos, Portugal.

75 Direcção Geral de Segurança, '*Acções das Nossas Forces*' Forces [Actions of Our Forces], DGS-Angola, 4 August 1971, SDGN 1802, Intelligence Report 963, Arquivo da Defesa Nacional, Paço do Arcos, Portugal.

76 Direcção Geral de Segurança, '*Acções das Nossas Forces*' [Actions of Our Forces], DGS-Angola, 11 August 1971, SDGN 1802, Intelligence Report 947, Arquivo da Defesa Nacional, Paço do Arcos, Portugal.

77 António Pires Nunes, *Siroco: Os Comandos no Leste de Angola* [Siroco: The Commandos in the East of Angola] (Lisbon: Assiciação de Comandos, 2013), pp. 364-422.

78 Direcção Geral de Segurança, Luanda, Angola, Cuanhamas–Political Subversion Situation], Intelligence Report 37/72-DINF-2ª, 8 July 1972, document F1.07.37.64, Arquivo da Defesa Nacional, Paço do Arcos, Portugal.

79 Direcção Geral de Segurança, '*Acções das Nossas Forces*' [Actions of Our Forces], DGS-Angola, 4 September 1971, SDGN 1802, Intelligence Report 1045, Arquivo da Defesa Nacional, Paço do Arcos, Portugal.

80 Direcção Geral de Segurança, '*Acções das Nossas Forces*' [Actions of Our Forces], DGS-Angola, 11 September 1971, SDGN 1802, Intelligence Report 1069, Arquivo da Defesa Nacional, Paço do Arcos, Portugal.

81 Ibid.

82 Ibid.

83 Ibid.

84 Direcção Geral de Segurança, '*Acções das Nossas Forces*' Forces [Actions of Our Forces], DGS-Angola, 22 June 1973, SDGN 1802, Intelligence Report 677, Arquivo da Defesa Nacional, Paço do Arcos, Portugal.

85 Ibid.

86 Direcção Geral de Segurança, '*Acções das Nossas Forces*' [Actions of Our Forces], DGS-Angola, 25 February 1972, SDGN 1802, Intelligence Report 260, Arquivo da Defesa Nacional, Paço do Arcos, Portugal.

87 Direcção Geral de Segurança, '*Acções das Nossas Forces*' [Actions of Our Forces], DGS-Angola, 31 March 1972, SDGN 1802, Intelligence Report 418, Arquivo da Defesa Nacional, Paço do Arcos, Portugal.

88 The DP-28 machine gun was an improvement from the earlier DP-26, both designed by Vasily Degtyaryov. The DP-28 was relatively cheap and easy to manufacture in that early models had fewer than 80 parts. The DP was especially able to withstand combat abuse, for in tests it was buried in sand and mud and, following its recovery, was still capable of firing more than 500 rounds. The DP was first supplemented in the 1950s by the more modern RPD machine gun and later in the 1960s entirely replaced in Soviet

service by the general purpose PK machine gun. Almost 800,000 copies of the DP-28 have been made since its introduction in 1928, and since the 1960s it has been supplied in significant quantities to pro-communist countries so that despite its obsolescence, it will be seen for many years.

89 Direcção Geral de Segurança, 'Acções das Nossas Forces' Forces [Actions of Our Forces], DGS-Angola, 27 March 1972, SDGN 1802, Intelligence Report 395, Arquivo da Defesa Nacional, Paço do Arcos, Portugal.

90 Direcção Geral de Segurança, 'Acções das Nossas Forces' [Actions of Our Forces], DGS-Angola, 31 March 1972, SDGN 1802, Intelligence Report 418, Arquivo da Defesa Nacional, Paço do Arcos, Portugal.

91 Engrácia dos Santos was one of the early political organizers in the MPLA.

92 Tala Hady is a village located in the province of Luanda, Angola, whose residents struggled "valiantly" against the Portuguese.

93 Joaquim Cardoso, 'Janguinda', was a director of the MPLA.

94 Teresa Afonso and Lucrécia Paim were heroines from the early years of the MPLA.

95 Direcção Geral de Segurança, 'Acções das Nossas Forces' [Actions of Our Forces], DGS-Angola, 5 April 1972, SDGN 1802, Intelligence Report 430, Arquivo da Defesa Nacional, Paço do Arcos, Portugal.

96 Direcção Geral de Segurança, 'Acções das Nossas Forces' [Actions of Our Forces], DGS-Angola, 23 June 1973, SDGN 1802, Intelligence Report 677, Arquivo da Defesa Nacional, Paço do Arcos, Portugal.

97 Ibid.

98 The Sterling sub-machine gun is a British weapon in service with the British Army from 1944 until 1994, when it was phased out. It fires 550 9mm Parabellum rounds per minute, weighs 6.0 pounds, and has a box clip of 34 rounds.

99 Ibid.

100 Ibid.

101 Direcção Geral de Segurança, 'Acções das Nossas Forces' [Actions of Our Forces], DGS-Angola, 10 July 1973, SDGN 1802, Intelligence Report 754, Arquivo da Defesa Nacional, Paço do Arcos, Portugal.

102 Ibid.

103 Ibid.

104 Direcção Geral de Segurança, 'Acções das Nossas Forces' [Actions of Our Forces], DGS-Angola, 25 June 1973, SDGN 1802, Intelligence Report 677, Arquivo da Defesa Nacional, Paço do Arcos, Portugal.

105 Tomás Francisco Ferreira was a commander in the MPLA areas in the north of Angola along the Congo frontier in 1961.

106 Direcção Geral de Segurança, 'Acções das Nossas Forces' [Actions of Our Forces], DGS-Angola, 18 July 1973, SDGN 1802, Intelligence Report 766, Arquivo da Defesa Nacional, Paço do Arcos, Portugal.

107 Hélio Felgas, 'Opinião' [Opinion], as quoted in Resenha Histórico-Militar das Campanhas de África, 1961–1974, 6th Volume, Tome I, Book 2, Angola by Comissão para o Estudo das Campanhas de África (1961–1974) (Lisbon: Estado-Maior do Exército, 2006), p. 450.

108 Ken Flower, Serving Secretly, Rhodesia's CIO Chief on Record (Alberton, South Africa: Galago Publishing, 1987), p. 300.

CHAPTER FIVE:
NEW FRONTIERS

The Flecha model of recruiting and training indigenous forces to operate in their home territory proved extremely effective in Angola, and hence there was a push to transfer this successful template to other theatres and other wars. In 1971, Óscar Cardoso was called by the PIDE/DGS Director, Fernando Silva Pais, and the Minister of the *Ultramar*, Joaquim da Silva Cunha, to organize Flechas in Mozambique.[1] To him this seemed ill-advised, as in Mozambique there already existed the Special Groups or *Grupos Especiais* (GEs) and the Special Groups Parachutists or *Grupos Especiais Pára-Quedistas* (GEPs), who were very good. These two groups were the brainchild of General Kaúlza de Arriaga, the Commander-in-Chief of the Armed Forces in Mozambique, and had been organized first as GEs in 1970. These were formed from service volunteers and later from captured insurgents or those who presented themselves. Their initial organization had consisted of six groups aggregating 550 men, and each group had the characteristics of the typical light infantry platoon or combat group. In 1971 GE training was extended to include a parachute qualification. The GEs eventually numbered about 7,700 men in 84 groups. The GEPs numbered about 840 men in 12 groups. Later there was a small number of Special Groups of Combat Trackers or *Grupos Especiais de Pisteiros de Combat* (GEPCs).[2] Thus, to Cardoso, not only did the Flechas seem superfluous, but the GEs were in direct competition for potential Flecha recruits. Consequently, he pursued other security duties for his assignment in Mozambique, establishing a system to detect and prevent FRELIMO infiltration.[3]

Flechas in Mozambique

Nevertheless, the notion of a Flecha-type force persisted. Ken Flower, head of the Rhodesian Central Intelligence Organization (CIO), argued that Flechas should be introduced into Mozambique; however, he experienced considerable resistance from the resident PIDE/DGS at the time for the nonsensical reason that PIDE/DGS in Angola had thought of it first.[4] In an attempt to overcome this pettiness and to better coordinate joint efforts in preventing insurgent infiltration in both Rhodesia and Mozambique, Flower spoke to Caetano in Lisbon in September 1971, again pushing to establish Flechas in Mozambique. It was argued that Arriaga was forming his GEs and that they should be adequate; however, Flower saw this as simply an extension of failed military strategy and unlikely to be the answer.[5] Later, in August 1972, Flower spoke once more with Caetano about an unconventional force. With the new appointment of Dr Aníbal São José Lopes as Joint Controller of PIDE/DGS operations for Angola and Mozambique, a belated move was made to introduce Flechas in Mozambique.

In early 1973, Captain Alvaro Manuel Alves Cardoso was chosen to begin recruiting and training such a force at Vila Pery, a city on the railway line, two-thirds of the way from the port of Beira on the Indian Ocean to the Rhodesian border. Alves Cardoso was an Angolan-born cavalry officer who had initially volunteered for the army and then for commando training. Subsequently, he proved himself in combat with a two-year tour in Guiné (1966–68) that left him a highly decorated hero. He had also held commando training assignments in Angola (1963–64) and at Lamego (1966) in the *metrópole*. At Vila Pery he initiated the commando-type training that he knew so well and had helped develop.

The Portuguese commando training course was one of the most rigorous of any army in the world. It lasted 15 weeks, and its volunteer recruits were subjected to an intense physical and psychological programme 24 hours a day. The theory behind this approach was that the action of war is not regulated by any particular day or any hour of the day. Thus, for example, Alves Cardoso might begin training exercises at 0200 and continue for several days unbroken. During his training there were no weekends, although periodically the trainees were given a day off. They were not told that the day was free but were able to rest without assignments, while waiting for their next order. During training, there was no established or predictable programme: candidates never knew what might happen next.

Instructors covered a wide array of topics, from political ideology to mines and booby traps, surveillance, intelligence-gathering, task organization and so on, and took great pains to stay abreast of the latest enemy operational methods and maintain the commando 'warrior edge'. As previously mentioned, this edge, in essence, was a philosophy of always acting as the hunter rather than the hunted. *Flechas* returning from contact with the enemy were debriefed and instructors regularly participated in operations to learn the latest enemy developments. This information or feed-back loop was integrated with intelligence from other sources gathered by military and national intelligence services, and the training was constantly revised to stay attuned to the enemy and his behaviour. This type of training had made the commandos a class apart, and would make the Flechas so too. Alves Cardoso's personal attention to the daily details of Flecha training reflected his desire to make them the best.

At the Vila Pery Flecha training facility, Alves Cardoso was visited in late 1973 by the commanding officer of the newly formed Rhodesian Selous Scouts Regiment, Major Ron Reid-Daly, who offered the following observation:

"His methods, tactics and training were ridiculously simple, yet perhaps because of this, very effective. His training syllabus for the unit consisted of repetitive training in basic skills that included fieldcraft, weapons handling, range work, and foot and arms drill on the parade square. Long hours were spent developing these skills, with pride of place being given to the rifle range.

"Between operations the whole unit spent its mornings on various firing ranges bulldozed into some hillsides. The range safety procedures were non-existent by Rhodesian standards. This was evidenced by the colonel [Captain Alves Cardoso], who would fire bursts of automatic fire from his favourite AK sub-machine gun past the ears, or at the feet, of any soldier he considered to be idle. But the results he obtained were quite outstanding and compared very favourably with any all-white Rhodesian regiment.

"The linchpin of all his training though was iron discipline.

"Imposing silence upon his men throughout the day impressed the supreme virtue of silence in the bush, perhaps the most important single item when conducting guerrilla operations. The only exception to this rule was when they were answering an instructor.

"Meals were eaten standing up. And woe betides any soldier careless enough to rattle a utensil, for retribution was swift in the form of a boot in the backside, a cane whacked down on the neck, or a hard punch to the ear!"[6]

Ultimately Alves Cardoso turned out about 200 Flechas allocated to seven combat groups: two in Vila Cabral, three in Téte, one in Beira and one in Vila Pery.

The Flechas operated in Mozambique for only two years, until the April 1974 Revolution. Supposedly, they were to be welcomed by the new FRELIMO government; however, in June, when all of the PIDE/DGS personnel were ordered imprisoned, they fled to Rhodesia. According to Reid-Daly, Alves Cardoso, together with the combat group and his recruits in training at Vila Pery, a total of 40 men, forced their way across the Mozambican border at gunpoint and made their way into Rhodesia. For a time Alves Cardoso and his Flechas served as a part of Reid-Daly's unit, for the Rhodesian army had hoped that enough Flechas would escape to form a company and that it could be used for cross-border operations to attack enemy bases in his Mozambican sanctuary. While a few more did arrive, news filtered into Rhodesia that large numbers of them had been either summarily shot or imprisoned by FRELIMO. Ultimately, the unit was disbanded, as there were never enough Flechas to man it fully. Further, the men seemed tired of fighting after having lost their country.[7]

Flechas in Guiné

In Guiné, from January 1972, there were a few small units of Flechas formed from locally recruited troops. Originally, these were designated Special Groups or *Grupos Especiais* (GEs). Sometime later these were redesignated Flechas and were considered the equivalent in capabilities of the Flechas in Angola. The Flecha programme in Guiné was, however, more *ad hoc* and far less structured. At the PIDE/DGS post in Cacine there was a GE unit of 13 men, of whom eleven had been recruited from the local militia and two from the civil population. At Bissorã there was a unit of six GEs, who were expert in infiltrating enemy units to gather intelligence and who also served as guides for military operations in the area. Their most noteworthy contribution occurred near Jagali, a village located seven miles due north of Bissorã. Here two GEs guided a force from Parachute Company 121 (*Companhia de Caçadores Paraquedistas Nº 121*) to a cache of war matériel that was captured intact without a shot being fired.[8]

Recruiting continued slowly, as first a single GE was recruited in Catió, then another 34 in August 1972 from the area around Cambajú, a village on the Senegalese border, 50 miles due north of Bafata. These latter recruits were aged between 19 and 34, 25 of whom came from the local militia, and nine from the surrounding civil population. In March 1974 ten more were recruited around Bissorã for actions against the PAIGC in the neighbouring areas of Tiligi, Biambe and Morés.[9]

This handful of GEs or Flechas had some notable successes. On 28 March 1972, some 17 Flechas operating around Cacoca on the southern frontier with Guiné-Conakry and just south of Cacine, recovered one anti-vehicle and 14 anti-personnel Soviet manufactured mines.[10] On 4 April, a contingent of Flechas was integrated with a force of marines (*Fuzileiros Navais*, or FNs) in an operation around Cantonaz, a village seven miles west of Catió on Colbert Island, where they successfully located a cache of war matériel.[11] The next day, 5 April, Flechas in the Cacine area killed 15 infiltrating PAIGC insurgents and captured diverse documents.[12] On 13 April, Flechas operating around Cacine discovered two Soviet anti-personnel mines.[13] Later, on 26 April, in a Flecha operation around Bissorã, several PAIGC insurgents were captured and 42 Soviet hand grenades were recovered.[14]

While the Flechas were useful, their numbers were small, and so their impact was limited. After the revolution, the new government promised amnesty to all Africans who had fought on the side of Portugal and invited them to stay on as citizens of the new country. No fewer than 27,000 accepted the offer; however, arrests of the former soldiers, sergeants and officers of the elite units began almost immediately, and their fate was inevitably execution. When questioned about these deaths, the new PAIGC leadership denied any wrongdoing. Ultimately, the newspaper *Nô Pintcha* published a partial list of names, and those who survived to escape estimate that at least a thousand faced firing squads, some at airfields, some at soccer fields and many in front of the civilian population.

Thus, for the valiant Flechas of Guiné, betrayal by their new government was a sad and final footnote.[15]

Flechas in South Africa

Guiné and Mozambique were not alone in their hypocrisy. Following the revolution in Lisbon in April 1974, it was decided that Portuguese forces would be withdrawn from Angola, and the country handed to the three nationalist organizations to sort out between themselves. It quickly became apparent that any Angolan who had been a loyal Portuguese soldier was on dangerous footing with the new authorities, particularly former members of elite forces and PIDE/DGS. The Bushmen, Flechas and their families were threatened. Between the revolution on 25 April and 2 November 1974, when the first group of 21 Flechas crossed the border into South Africa, fully armed and prepared to fight their way out, Flecha family after family was murdered in a series of massacres by the 'liberation movements'.[6] In one case, over 130 Bushmen were shot in a bloody genocidal bout at Mavinga.[17] Later, it was estimated that fully 25 per cent of all Angolan Bushmen were killed in this seven-month period.[18] Eventually, enough Angolan Flechas escaped to form a company in the SADF, initially known as Combat Group Alpha. Following Operation Savannah (September 1975–January 1976), it was renamed 31 Battalion. Later, in 1979, its name was again changed to 201 Battalion, and expanded with Bushmen from the Caprivi Strip, Ovamboland, and South West Africa. 31 Battalion continued the tradition of excellence established in Angola under the Portuguese until its deactivation in September 2011. The performance of the Flechas in both the Angolan and South African theatres is well encapsulated in a note from Captain Francisco José de Morais, commanding officer of Cavalry Battalion 2870, to Óscar Cardoso. This unit operated with the Flechas shoulder-to-shoulder in Cuando Cubango (CC) over an 18-month period, culminating in November 1970: "And permit me, Your Excellency, to cite the special task force that evolved into the marvellous experience of knowing and subsequently living and fighting side by side with your great and valiant warriors, the Flechas, during operations in Sector CC."[19]

When the South African Border War ended in 1989, civilization had taken its toll on the Bushmen, as Elizabeth Thomas observes:

"Many people under 30 hardly remembered the old way of life. Others remembered but had forgotten the skills necessary to lead it. Even people in their forties who knew some of the skills lacked the fine knowledge that everyone once had. Only the old people remembered everything, and it was they who best realized what had been lost. Nowadays, perhaps not surprisingly, they seldom discuss the past."[20]

1 Óscar Cardoso, '*Criador dos Flechas*' [Creator of the Flechas] in José Freire Antunes, *A Guerra de África, 1961–1974, Volume 1* [The War in Africa, 1961–1974, Volume 1] (Lisbon: Temas e Debates, 1996), p. 412.

2 Comissão para o Estudo das Campanhas de África, *Resenha Histórico-Militar das Campanhas de África 1961–1974, Tomo I, Enquadramento Geral* [Historical Military Report on the African Campaigns 1961–1974, Tome I, General Situation] (Lisbon: Estado-Maior de Exército, 1988), pp. 242-4.

3 Óscar Cardoso, p. 412.

4 Ken Flower, *Serving Secretly, Rhodesia's CIO Chief on Record* (Alberton, South Africa: Galago Publishing, 1987), p. 300.

5 Ibid.

6 R.F. Reid-Daly, *Pamwe Chete: The Legend of the Selous Scouts* (Johannesburg: Covos Day, 2001), p. 61.

7 Ibid, p. 62.

8 IAN/TT, Arquivos de PIDE, Torre do Tombo, Lisbon, Processo 7.477-CI(2), Comando de Operações, pasta 29, Letter to Dircetor General of Security from Fragoso Allas, Adjunct Inspector, DGS, 27 January 1972, subject: Flechas/Guiné, pp. 37-9.

9 Ibid.

10 Ibid, pp. 19-20.

11 Ibid, p. 17.

12 Ibid, p. 16.

13 Ibid, p. 19.

14 Ibid, p. 13.

15 Eduardo Dâmaso and Adelino Gomes, '*Falecidos por Fuzilamento*' [Death by Shooting], *Pública* (30 June 1996), p. 48.

16 Ian Uys, *Bushman Soldiers, Their Alpha and Omega* (Germiston, South Africa: Fortress Publishers, 1993), p. 11.

17 Ibid.

18 Ibid.

19 Letter from Captain Francisco José do Morais, commanding officer, Cavalry Battalion 2870, to Inspector Óscar Cardoso, Sub-Delegation of the DGS, Serpa Pinto, Angola, 5 November 1970, Military Region of Angola Note 3485/70 REAB, personal archive of Óscar Cardoso.

20 Elizabeth Marshall Thomas, *The Harmless People* (New York: Vintage Books, 1989), pp. 282-3.

BIBLIOGRAPHY

Portuguese Government Publications & Documents

Estado-Maior do Exército. *Resenha Histórico-Militar das Campanhas de* África, *Vols. I–V.* [Historical Military Report of the African Campaigns, Vol. I–V]. Lisbon: Estado-Maior do Exército, 1989.

Interviews & Correspondence

Cardoso, Óscar. Inspector, *Polícia Internacional e de Defesa do Estado* (PIDE) and its successor, *Direcção Geral de Segurança* (DGS), from 1965 to 1974. Interviews by the author, 1 April 1995, Azaruja, Portugal, and 18 June 2012, Casal do Mogos, Santo Isidoro, Portugal.

Background Literature

Abshire, David M. & Samuels, Michael A. *Portuguese Africa, A Handbook*. New York: Praeger Publishers, 1969.

Afonso, Aniceto & Gomes, Carlos de Matos. *Guerra Colonial.* [Colonial War]. Lisbon: Notícias, 1998.

Antunes, José Freire.

Armstrong, Sue. *In Search of Freedom*. Gibraltar: Ashanti Publishing, 1989.

Borges Coelho, João Paulo. 'African Troops in the Portuguese Colonial Army, 1961–1974: Angola, Guinea-Bissau and Mozambique'. *Portuguese Studies Review* (Spring–Summer 2002): pp. 129–50.

Bruce, Neil. 'Portugal's African Wars'. *Conflict Studies* 34 (March 1973): pp. 1–22.

Cabral, Amílcar. *Guiné-Bissau–Nação Africana Forjada na Luta.* [Guiné-Bissau–African Nation Forged in Struggle]. Lisbon: Publicações Nova Auora, 1974.

_____. *Textos Políticos.* [Political Texts]. Porto: Edições Afrontamento, 1974.

_____. *Palavras de Ordem Gerais.* [Speeches on Overall Methods]. Bissau: PAIGC/Secretariado Geral, 1976.

Cann, John P. *Contra-Subversão em África.* [Counterinsurgency in Africa]. Lisbon: Prefácio, 2005.

Cardoso, Óscar Cardoso. 'Criador dos Flechas'. [Creator of the Flechas]. In José Freire Antunes, *A Guerra de* África, *1961–1974, Volume 1.* [The War in Africa, 1961–1974, Volume 1]. Lisbon: Temas e Debates, 1996.

Castanheira, José Pedro. 'Ao Serviço de Spínola e Marcelo'. [In the Service of Spínola e Marcelo]. *Expresso*, 20 September 1997, p. 56.

_____. 'Memórias da Guerra e da Paz: Spínola'. [Memories of War and Peace: Spínola]. *Expresso Revista*, 30 April 1994, p. 26.

Caetano, Marcello. *Depoimento.* [Deposition]. Rio de Janeiro: Distribuidora Record, 1974.

Cardoso, Edgar Pereira da Costa. *Presença da Força Aérea em Angola.* [Presence of the Air Force in Angola]. Lisbon: Secretaria de Estado de Aeronáutica, 1963.

Chabal, Patrick. *Amílcar Cabral*. Cambridge: Cambridge University Press, 1983.

Clarence-Smith, W. Gervase. *The Third Portuguese Empire 1825–1975: A Study in Economic Imperialism*. Manchester: Manchester University Press, 1985.

Dâmaso, Eduardo & Gomes, Adelino. 'Falecidos por Fuzilamento'. [Death by Shooting]. *Pública*, 30 June 1996, p. 48.

Felgas, Hélio. *Os Movimentos Terroristas.* [The Terrorist Movements]. Lisbon: Privately printed, 1966.

_____. *Guerra em Angola.* [War in Angola]. Lisbon: Livraria Clássica Editora, 1961.

_____. *O Clima do Congo Português.* [The Climate of Portuguese Congo]. Carmona: Imprensa Angolana, 1959.

Gleijeses, Piero. *Conflicting Missions: Havana, Washington, and Africa, 1959–1976*. Chapel Hill: University of North Carolina Press, 2002.

Lima Bacelar, Sérgio Augusto Margarido. *A Guerra em* África *1961–1974: Estratégias Adoptadas pelas Forças Armadas.* [The War in Africa 1961–1974: Strategies Adopted by the Armed Forces]. Porto: Liga dos Amigos do Museu Militar do Porto and Universidade Portucalenese Infante D. Henrique, 2000.

Marcum, John. *The Angolan Revolution. Volume 1, The Anatomy of an Explosion (1950–1962)*. Cambridge: M.I.T. Press, 1969.

Mateus, Dalila Cabrita. *A PIDE/DGS na Guerra Colonial 1961–1974.* [The PIDE/DGS in the Colonial War 1961–1974]. Lisbon: Terramar, 2004.

Mondlane, Eduardo. *The Struggle for Mozambique*. London: Zed Press, 1969.

Newett, Malyn. *A History of Mozambique*. London: Hurst & Co., 1995.

_____. *Portugal in Africa: The Last Hundred Years*. London: C. Hurst & Co., 1981.

Nogueira e Carvalho, José Victor de Brito. *Era Tempo de Morrer em* África: *Angola, Guerra e Descolonização, 1961–1975.* [It Was a Time to Die in Africa: Angola, War and Decolonization, 1961–1975]. Lisbon: Prefácio, 2004.

Pélissier, René. *Naissance de la Guiné, Portugais et Africains en Sénégambie (1841–1936)*. Orgeval: Pélissier, 1989.

_____. *Naissance du Mozambique: Résistance et Révoltes Anticoloniales (1854–1918)*. Orgeval: Pélissier, 1984.

_____. *Le Naufrage des Caravelles, Etudes sur la Fin de l'Empire Portugais (1961–1975)*. Orgeval: Editions Pélissier, 1979.

_____. *La Colonie du Minotaure, Nationalismes et Révoltes en Angola (1926–1961)*. Orgeval: Editions Pélissier, 1978.

Petter-Bowyer, Peter J.H. *Winds of Destruction*. Victoria: Trafford, 2003.

Pezarat Correia, Pedro. 'A Participação Local no Desenvolvimento das Campanhas: O Reucrutamento Africano'. [Local Participation in the Expansion of the Campaigns]. In *Estudos sobre as Campanhas de África (1961–1974)*. [Studies on the African Campaigns]. Instituto de Altos Estudos Militares, ed. São Pedro Estoril: Edições Atena, 2000.

Pires Nunes, António. *Siroco: Os Comandos no Leste de Angola*. [Siroco: The Comandos in the East of Angola]. Lisbon: Associação de Comandos, 2013.

_____. *Angola 1966–1974, Vitória Militar no Leste*. [Angola 1966–1974, Military Victory in the East]. Lisbon: Prefácio, 2002.

Porch, Douglas. *The Portuguese Armed Forces and the Revolution*. Stanford: The Hoover Institution Press, 1977.

Reid-Daly, Ron F. *Pamwe Chete: The Legend of the Selous Scouts*. Johannesburg: Covos Day, 2001.

Robinson, Richard. *Contemporary Portugal*. London: George Allen & Unwin, 1979.

Rodrigues, Luís Nuno. *Salazar–Kennedy: A Crise de uma Aliança*. [Salazar–Kennedy: The Crisis of an Alliance]. Lisbon: Editorial Notícias, 2002.

Silva Cunha, Joaquim Moreira da. *O Ultramar, a Nação e o '25 de Abril'*. [The Overseas Provinces, the Nation and the '25th of April']. Coimbra: Atlântida Editora, 1977.

Spínola, António de. *Portugal e o Futuro*. [Portugal and the Future]. Lisbon: Editoria Arcádia, 1974.

Steenkamp, Willem. *South Africa's Border War, 1966–1989*. Gibraltar: Ashanti Publishing, 1989.

Uys, Ian. *Bushman Soldiers, Their Alpha and Omega*. Germiston, South Africa: Fortress Publishers, 1993.

van der Waals, W. S.. *Portugal's War in Angola 1961–1974*. Rivonia: Ashanti, 1993.

Wheeler, Douglas L. & Pélissier, René. *Angola*. London: Pall Mall Press, 1971.

Acknowledgements

This book would not have been possible without the unstinting support of my long-time friend, Óscar Cardoso, former inspector with the Portuguese security service who, in 1966, had the vision to develop the Bushmen of southeastern Angola into a formidable armed reconnaissance and intelligence-gathering force. I am most thankful for the generous support and time that he gave me.

I am also deeply indebted to my long-time friend, João José Brandão Ferreira, who helped me find my way around rural Portugal, as well as the *Arquivo da Defesa Nacional in Paço do Arcos*. I am equally indebted to my dear friend Clemente Fernandes Gil, who also helped me at the *Arquivo da Defesa Nacional*. Likewise, I am deeply appreciative of the patience and professionalism of the staff at the *Arquivo da Defesa Nacional,* all of whom helped me, with wonderful efficiency, to locate and uncover material on the Flechas and made suggestions as to where additional useful records might be found.

Jaime Ferreira Regalado and I spent many hours sharing a mutual interest in the Flechas, and I am most appreciative of our time together.

Finally, I owe a particular debt to my wife Anne, who lived patiently with the domestic chaos of this work.

John P. Cann is a Research Fellow at Marine Corps University, a former member of the research staff at the Institute for Defence Analyses, a former Scholar-in-Residence at the University of Virginia, and the retired Professor of National Security Studies at Marine Corps University. He earned his doctorate in the Department of War Studies at King's College London in 1996 and subsequently published *Counterinsurgency in Africa: The Portuguese Way of War, 1961–1974* and *Brown Waters of Africa: Portuguese Riverine Warfare, 1961–1974*. He is likewise the author of some thirty articles on conflict in Africa. He is a retired naval captain and flight officer specializing in open-ocean-reconnaissance aviation with a variety of aviation assignments, including command. He also served on the staffs of the Chief of Naval Operations and the Secretary of Defence and was awarded the Portuguese Medal of Dom Afonso Henriques and the Portuguese Navy Cross Medal. He is an Associate Member of the Academia de Marinha.